Happy Holidays in PLASTIC CANVAS

Edited by Laura Scott

HOUSE of
WHITE
BIRCHES
PUBLISHERS
SINCE 1947

Editor: Laura Scott
Associate Editor: June Sprunger
Copy Editor: Cathy Reef
Photography: Tammy Christian, Nancy Sharp
Cover Photography: Tammy Cromer-Campbell
Photography Assistants: Linda Quinlan, Arlou Wittwer

Production Manager: Vicki Macy
Creative Coordinator: Shaun Venish
Book and Cover Design/Production: Dan Kraner
Traffic Coordinator: Sandra Beres
Production Assistants: Carol Dailey, Cheryl Lynch, Jessica Rothe, Dana Brotherton, Miriam Zacharias

Publishers: Carl H. Muselman, Arthur K. Muselman
Chief Executive Officer: John Robinson
Marketing Director: Scott Moss
Editorial Director: Vivian Rothe
Production Director: George Hague

Printed in the United States of America
First Printing: 1998
Library of Congress Number: 98-070677
ISBN: 1-882138-37-6

A Note From the Editor

It used to be that most people decorated primarily for Christmas and not so much for the other holidays of the year. Have you noticed in recent years that many people make a point of celebrating all the holidays of the year?

People today are living life to the fullest, and for many this means making the most of all these annual festive occasions. From special gifts for friends, co-workers and family, to cheery decorations at home or the office, bright and colorful holiday accents are popping up everywhere!

It is my hope that this book of more than 90 projects will become one that you use again and again when looking for the perfect project for New Year's Day, Valentine's Day, St. Patrick's Day, Easter, Mother's and Father's Days, Independence Day, Halloween, Thanksgiving, and Hanukkah or Christmas.

From Jan. 1 through Dec. 31, my staff and I wish you many hours of pleasant stitching, sharing and decorating!

Warm regards,

Laura Scott

Laura Scott, editor
Happy Holidays in Plastic Canvas

CONTENTS

All-American Celebration

Happy Halloween

A Day of Thanks

Happy Hanukkah

Merry Christmas

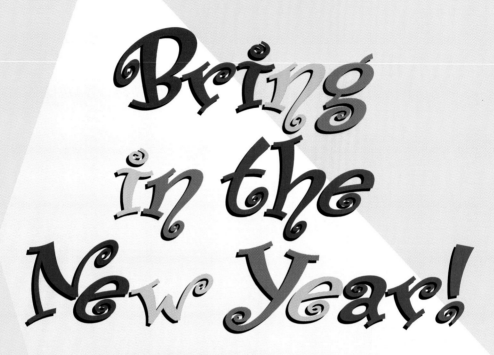

Bring in the New Year!

Get the new year off to a great start with this collection of terrific projects sure to keep you in stitches from now to the year 2000 and beyond! From bright and bold noise-makers to an inspirational calendar holder, these projects will make your New Year's Eve celebrations the best ever!

Celebration Sign

Welcome your New Year's party guests into your home with this colorful party sign! With its bright, festive design, you'll want to use it year after year!

Design by Carol Nartowicz • Shown on page 7

Skill Level: Beginner

Materials

- 1 sheet clear 7-count plastic canvas
- 1 sheet white 7-count plastic canvas
- Uniek Needloft plastic canvas yarn as listed in color key
- 14" each Uniek Needloft metallic craft cord: gold #01, blue #02, red #03, green #04, turquoise #05, cerise #06
- Satin ribbon:
  8" ⅜"-wide purple
  8" ¼"-wide bright yellow
  8" ⅛"-wide green
  8" ⅛"-wide royal
- 2 (8" x 10") pieces fusible fleece
- Monofilament
- Hot-glue gun

Instructions

1. Cut sign front from white plastic canvas and sign back and masks from clear plastic canvas according to graphs. Sign back will remain unstitched.

2. Place fusible fleece on backside of front. Stitch front through fleece following graph. Place second piece of fleece between front and back pieces; Whipstitch front and back together with white.

3. Stitch masks following graph. Overcast inside and outside edges with black.

4. Using photo (page 7) as a guide through step 6, place gold, turquoise and cerise cord together. Fold over one end of bunch 1¾"; tack bottom of fold to left side of one mask with monofilament. Repeat with blue, red and green cord, tacking bottom of fold to right side of second mask.

5. Glue first mask to upper left corner and second mask to lower right corner of sign front.

6. Matching colors, thread ribbon under balloons from front to back through holes indicated on graph. Knot ends on backside of sign. Curl ribbon as desired, gluing each loop to sign front.

7. Hang as desired. ❖

COLOR KEY	
Plastic Canvas Yarn	**Yards**
■ Black #00	7
■ Christmas red #02	3
▥ Tangerine #11	1
■ Christmas green #28	1
▨ Royal #32	1
■ Bright purple #64	1
⁄ White #41 Whipstitching	4
● Attach ribbon	
Color numbers given are for Uniek Needloft plastic canvas yarn.	

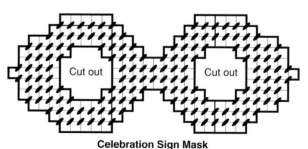

Celebration Sign Mask
28 holes x 11 holes
Cut 2 from clear

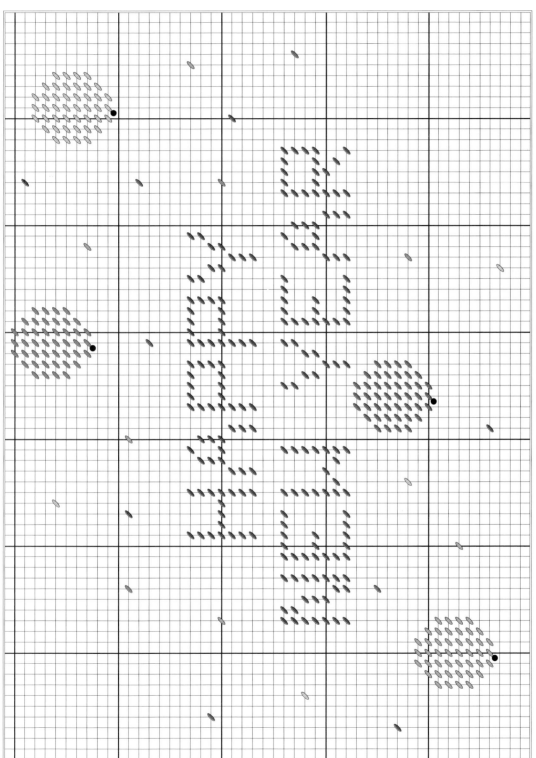

Celebration Sign Front & Back
70 holes x 51 holes
Cut 1 front from white, stitch as graphed
Cut 1 back from clear, do not stitch

New Year's

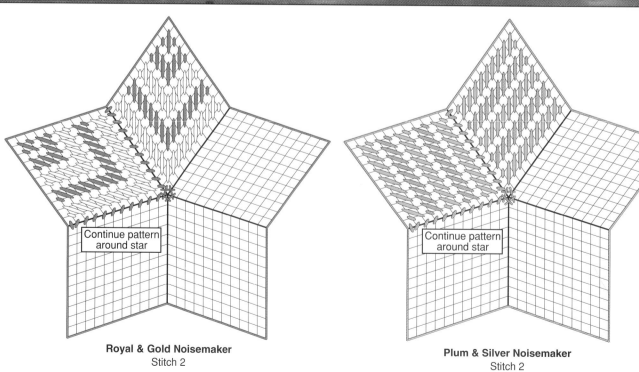

Royal & Gold Noisemaker
Stitch 2

Continue pattern around star

Plum & Silver Noisemaker
Stitch 2

Continue pattern around star

Noisemakers

Bring in the new year with this collection of fun and festive noisemakers! With their bright colors and loud noises, they're sure to be a hit at your countdown party!

Designs by Angie Arickx

Skill Level: Beginner

Materials

- 6 (5") plastic canvas stars by Uniek
- Uniek Needloft plastic canvas yarn as listed in color key
- ⅛"-wide Plastic Canvas 7 Metallic Needlepoint Yarn by Rainbow Gallery as listed in color key
- #16 tapestry needle
- Plastic or wooden beads, marbles or jingle bells

Instructions

1. Cut tabs from plastic canvas stars, then stitch following graphs.

2. With wrong sides together and with points of each star between the other star's points, Whipstitch two rainbow stars together with purple, placing beads, marbles or jingle bells inside before completing Whipstitching.

3. Repeat step 2 for remaining noisemakers, Whipstitching plum-and-silver stars together with plum and royal-and-gold stars together with royal. ❖

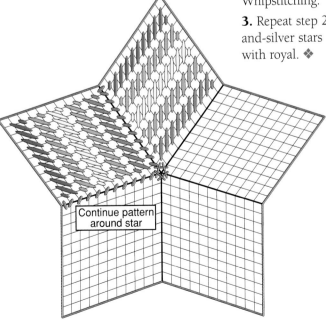

Rainbow Noisemaker
Stitch 2

COLOR KEY	
Plastic Canvas Yarn	**Yards**
■ Christmas red #02	5
■ Royal #32	20
■ Purple #46	6
■ Mermaid #53	5
☐ Yellow #57	5
■ Bright orange #58	5
■ Plum #59	15
⁄ Royal #32 Backstitch	
⁄ Purple #46 Backstitch	
⁄ Plum #59 Backstitch	
⅛" Metallic Needlepoint Yarn	
☐ Gold #PC1	11
■ Silver #PC2	11
Color numbers given are for Uniek Needloft plastic canvas yarn and Rainbow Gallery Plastic Canvas 7 Metallic Needlepoint Yarn.	

Design by Vicki Blizzard

*Make the new year more meaningful by meeting your resolutions,
and more attractive by stitching this inspirational calendar holder!*

Skill Level: Beginner

Materials

- 2 sheets 7-count plastic canvas
- Uniek Needloft plastic canvas yarn as listed in color key
- DMC #3 pearl cotton as listed in color key
- #16 tapestry needle
- 8 (6mm) round gold beads from The Beadery
- 15 (4mm) ruby round faceted beads from The Beadery
- 10 (6mm) translucent petal pink baby's breath flower beads from The Beadery
- 9 (12mm) translucent rose dogwood flower beads from The Beadery
- Mill Hill Products glass seed beads from Gay Bowles

Sales, Inc.:
10 pink #02018
45 yellow #02002
- Clear thread
- Beading needle
- Sawtooth hanger
- Hot-glue gun

Instructions

1. Cut plastic canvas according to graph. Calendar holder back will remain unstitched.

2. Stitch calendar holder front following graph, working uncoded area with eggshell Continental Stitches. Work pearl cotton embroidery over completed background stitching.

3. Using beading needle and clear thread through step 5, attach gold beads where indicated

on graph. For ruby beads, bring needle up in hole indicated on graph, thread on three beads and bring needle down through the same hole. Tack down circle of beads so they lie flat. Repeat for remaining ruby beads.

4. For translucent petal pink flowers, bring needle up where indicated on graph, thread needle through hole on one flower, then thread on one pink seed bead. Bring needle down through hole in flower and same hole in plastic canvas. Repeat for remaining pink flowers.

5. For translucent rose flowers, repeat step 4, threading on five yellow seed beads in center of each flower.

6. Whipstitch holder front to holder back around inside and

Calendar Holder Front & Back
90 holes x 42 holes
Cut 2, stitch 1

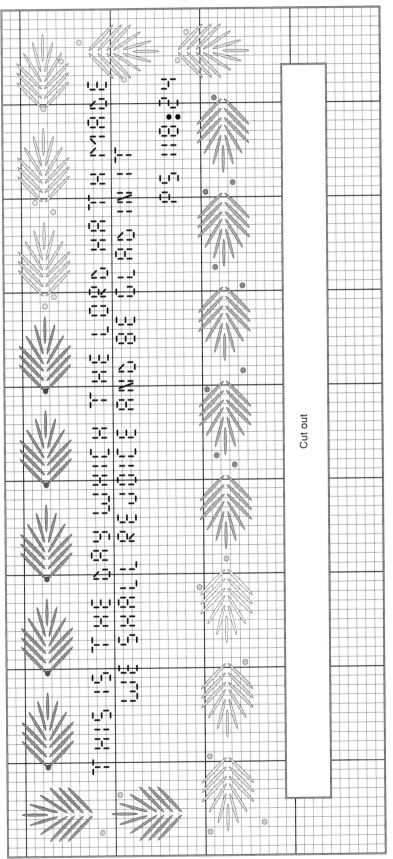

outside edges with forest. Glue
sawtooth hanger to center top
on holder back. ❖

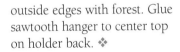

COLOR KEY

Plastic Canvas Yarn	Yards
▨ Rust #09	1
▨ Sundown #10	1
▢ Pumpkin #12	1
▢ Straw #19	1
▢ Moss #25	3
▨ Holly #27	3
▨ Forest #29	9
▢ Yellow #57	1
Uncoded area is eggshell #39	
Continental Stitches	52

#3 Pearl Cotton

╱ Ultra dark pistachio green #890 Backstitch	7
● Ultra dark pistachio green #890 French Knot	
○ Attach gold bead	
● Attach ruby bead	
○ Attach translucent petal pink flower	
● Attach translucent rose flower	

Color numbers given are for Uniek Needloft plastic
canvas yarn and DMC #3 pearl cotton.

New Year's Fridgies

Designs by Mary T. Cosgrove

Celebrate the newness of 1999 with this set of three colorful fridgies! Use them to tack resolutions and reminders to your refrigerator or filing cabinet!

Skill Level: Beginner

Materials

- ⅓ sheet Uniek Quick-Count 7-count plastic canvas
- Uniek Needloft plastic canvas yarn as listed in color key
- #16 tapestry needle
- ½" magnetic strip
- Craft glue

Instructions

1. Cut plastic canvas according to graphs.

2. Stitch pieces following graphs. Overcast banner with pink, hat with turquoise and bright yellow and party favor with bright pink and bright yellow following graphs.

3. Cut a 6" length of pink yarn. Thread ends from front to back through holes indicated with black dots on party hat graph; knot ends.

4. Cut two pieces magnetic strip to fit back of each stitched piece. Glue in place. ❖

COLOR KEY	
Plastic Canvas Yarn	**Yards**
▨ Turquoise #54	4
▧ Bright pink #62	8
☐ Bright yellow #63	5
Color numbers given are for Uniek Needloft plastic canvas yarn.	

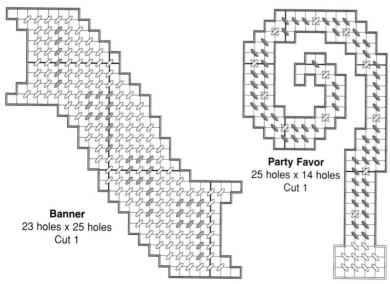

Banner
23 holes x 25 holes
Cut 1

Party Favor
25 holes x 14 holes
Cut 1

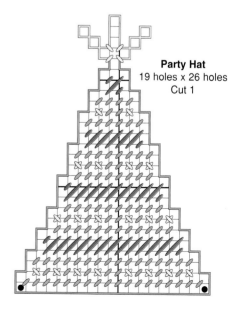

Party Hat
19 holes x 26 holes
Cut 1

Valentine's Day Delights

Treats and sweets for your sweet are in order this Valentine's Day! From darling magnets for leaving a love note on the fridge to mini candy baskets and more, you'll find just the right way to stitch "I love you"!

Precious Pet Treat Baskets

Designs by Vicki Blizzard

Don't forget your furry friends this Valentine's Day! Delight all your loving critters with their own special treats!

Skill Level: Beginner

Materials

Each Basket

- 1 sheet 7-count plastic canvas
- 4½" radial circle
- #16 tapestry needle
- Spinrite plastic canvas yarn as listed in color key
- Sewing needle and clear thread
- Hot-glue gun

Precious Puppy

- DMC 6-strand embroidery floss as listed in color key
- Sheet red felt
- Red sewing thread

- 3 (6mm) round black cabochons
- 1½ yards ⅛"-wide light blue satin ribbon

Precious Kitten

- DMC 6-strand embroidery floss: 1" white and as listed in color key
- Sheet medium pink felt
- Pink sewing thread
- 2 (6mm) round black cabochons
- 2 (¼") white pompoms
- 3mm pink pompom
- 1½ yards ⅛"-wide light pink satin ribbon

Precious Lovebird

- Sheet white felt
- White sewing thread
- 2 (6mm) round black cabochons
- 1½ yards ⅛"-wide yellow satin ribbon

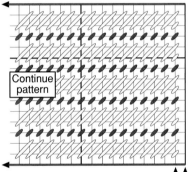

Treat Basket Side
90 holes x 15 holes
Cut 1 for each basket
Stitch as graphed for puppy basket
Replace scarlet with cherry blossom
for kitten basket
Replace scarlet with candy
for lovebird basket

Treat Basket Heart Body
17 holes x 16 holes
Cut 1 for each basket
Stitch puppy body as graphed
Stitch kitten body with cherry blossom
Stitch lovebird body with candy

Treat Basket Small Heart
7 holes x 7 holes
Cut 2 for each basket
Stitch as graphed for puppy basket
Replace scarlet with cherry blossom
for kitten basket
Replace scarlet with candy
for lovebird basket

Treat Basket Handle
3 holes x 70 holes
Cut 1 for each basket
Stitch as graphed for puppy basket
Replace scarlet with cherry blossom
for kitten basket
Replace scarlet with candy
for lovebird basket

Baskets

1. For each basket, cut one basket side, one handle, two small hearts and one heart body from plastic canvas according to graphs (page 17). Cut one row off outside edge of each 4½" circle for basket bottoms. Basket bottoms will remain unstitched.

2. Stitch puppy basket, handle, small hearts and body heart following graphs. Overlap side edges of basket where indicated on graph; stitch overlap with Continental Stitches, continuing with colors in pattern. Using scarlet throughout, Overcast handle, hearts and top edge of basket. Whipstitch basket bottom to bottom edge of basket side.

3. For basket lining, cut a 9" circle from red felt. With red sewing thread and needle, sew a Running Stitch ⅛" from outside edge of circle. Pull Running Stitch to form a pouch that fits inside basket, adjusting gathers evenly. Sew lining in place with clear sewing thread.

4. Stitch and line kitten basket following steps 2 and 3, replacing scarlet yarn with cherry blossom yarn and red felt with medium pink felt. Repeat for lovebird basket, replacing scarlet yarn with candy yarn and red felt with white felt.

5. With seam at the back, glue handles to basket sides. Glue one small heart to each end of handle.

6. For puppy basket, cut three 12" lengths of light blue ribbon. Hold all three pieces together and tie in a bow; trim ends. Glue bow to top of handle. Cut remaining ribbon into three 6" lengths. Tie each piece into a small bow; trim ends. Glue one bow to bottom of each small heart. Set remaining bow aside until basket is completed.

7. Repeat step 6 for remaining two baskets, using corresponding ribbons for each basket.

Precious Puppy

1. Cut puppy pieces from plastic canvas according to graphs.

2. Stitch pieces following graphs. With wrong sides together, Whipstitch dart on each ear together with black; Overcast remaining edges. Overcast head, muzzle and paws with white. Overcast tail and feet with black.

3. Work embroidery on paws and muzzle with 6 strands floss. Work French Knots on feet with pale pink yarn.

4. Using photo as a guide through step 6, center and glue muzzle to head, making sure bottom edges are even. Glue one ear to each upper side of head. Glue one cabochon to muzzle for nose where indicated on graph. Glue remaining two cabochons to head for eyes.

5. Center and glue head at a slight angle to back of scarlet body heart along top edge. Glue one paw to each upper side of heart front. Glue one foot to each bottom side of heart front. Glue tail to back of heart on right side. Glue remaining light blue bow to front of heart directly under head.

6. Glue assembled puppy to basket front, making sure bottom edges are even.

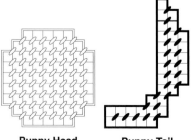

Puppy Head
9 holes x 9 holes
Cut 1

Puppy Tail
8 holes x 12 holes
Cut 1

COLOR KEY
PRECIOUS PUPPY

Plastic Canvas Yarn	Yards
☐ White #0001	18
☐ Pale pink #0003	1
■ Black #0028	3
■ Scarlet #0022	15
○ Pale pink #0003 French Knot	

6-Strand Embroidery Floss

╱ Black #310 Backstitch and Straight Stitch	1
● Black #310 French Knot	
● Attach black nose cabochon	

Color numbers given are for Spinrite plastic canvas yarn and DMC 6-strand embroidery floss.

Puppy Muzzle
7 holes x 4 holes
Cut 1

Puppy Foot
4 holes x 5 holes
Cut 2

Join

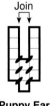

Puppy Ear
3 holes x 6 holes
Cut 2

Puppy Paw
5 holes x 4 holes
Cut 2

Precious Kitten

1. Cut kitten pieces from plastic canvas according to graphs (page 19). Ears will remain unstitched.

2. Stitch pieces following graphs, Overcasting tail with gray and white while stitching. With right sides together, Whipstitch dart on each ear together with silver gray; Overcast remaining edges. Overcast paws with white. Overcast head and feet with silver gray.

3. Work Straight Stitches on paw with 6 strands floss. Work French Knots on feet with pale pink yarn.

4. Using photo as a guide through step 6, glue two white pompoms to head for muzzle.

COLOR KEY
PRECIOUS KITTEN

Plastic Canvas Yarn	Yards
☐ White #0001	17
☐ Pale pink #0003	1
Cherry blossom #0010	15
☐ Silver gray #0045	3
○ Pale pink #0003 French Knot	
6-Strand Embroidery Floss	
✓ Black #310 Backstitch and Straight Stitch	½
● Black #310 French Knot	

Color numbers given are for Spinrite plastic canvas yarn and DMC 6-strand embroidery floss.

Join

Kitten Ear
3 holes x 2 holes
Cut 2
Do not stitch

Kitten Foot
4 holes x 5 holes
Cut 2

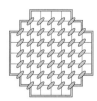

Kitten Head
8 holes x 8 holes
Cut 1

Kitten Paw
5 holes x 4 holes
Cut 2

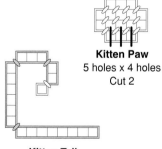

Kitten Tail
9 holes x 8 holes
Cut 1

Glue center of 1" length white floss to center top of muzzle. Glue pink pompom over floss for nose. Unravel floss ends to form whiskers. Glue cabochons to head for eyes.

5. Glue one ear to each upper side of head. Center and glue head at a slight angle to back of cherry blossom body heart along top edge. Glue one paw to each

upper side of heart front. Glue one foot to each bottom side of heart front. Glue tail to back of heart on left side. Glue remaining light pink bow to front of heart directly under head.

6. Glue assembled kitten to basket front, making sure bottom edges are even.

Precious Lovebird

1. Cut lovebird pieces from plastic canvas according to graphs. One beak piece (beak back) will remain unstitched.

2. Stitch pieces following graphs, reversing one wing before stitching. Overcast head and wings with clover and feet with daffodil.

3. Using daffodil throughout, Overcast two adjacent edges of one stitched beak from dot to dot. Repeat with second stitched beak. Whipstitch

COLOR KEY
PRECIOUS LOVEBIRD

Plastic Canvas Yarn	Yards
☐ White #0001	15
☐ Peach #0007	1
Candy #0025	15
☐ Daffodil #0029	2
☐ Clover #0042	2

Color numbers given are for Spinrite plastic canvas yarn.

Lovebird Wing
5 holes x 4 holes
Cut 2, reverse 1

Lovebird Foot
5 holes x 5 holes
Cut 2

remaining two edges of one stitched beak to two edges of beak back. Repeat with second stitched beak and remaining edges of beak back.

4. Using photo as a guide throughout step 6, cut a 4" length of green and attach to backside of head at center top, leaving ends free above top of head. Unravel ends and trim to 1".

5. Glue beak to head between cheeks. Glue cabochons to head for eyes. Center and glue head at a slight angle to back of candy body heart along top edge. Glue one wing to each upper side of heart front. Glue one foot to each bottom side of heart front. Glue remaining yellow bow to front of heart directly under head.

6. Glue assembled lovebird to basket front, making sure bottom edges are even. ❖

Lovebird Beak
3 holes x 3 holes
Cut 3, stitch 2

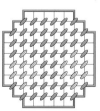

Lovebird Head
9 holes x 9 holes
Cut 1

Conversation Hearts Basket

Design by Michele Wilcox

Fill this colorful Valentine basket with candy hearts or chocolate kisses to share with your family or co-workers this Valentine's Day!

Skill Level: Beginner

Materials

- 1½ sheets 7-count plastic canvas
- Uniek Needloft plastic canvas yarn as listed in color key
- DMC #3 pearl cotton as listed in color key
- Hot-glue gun

Instructions

1. Cut plastic canvas according to graphs.

2. Stitch pieces following graphs, working uncoded areas with crimson Continental Stitches. Work Backstitches with pearl cotton when background stitching is completed.

3. Overcast top straight edges on sides beneath lace with crimson. Using white throughout, Overcast lace handle and lace on top edges of sides. Whipstitch sides together, then Whipstitch sides to bottom.

4. Center and glue handle inside basket long sides. ❖

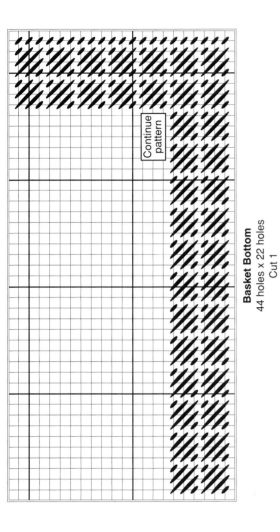

Basket Bottom
44 holes x 22 holes
Cut 1

Continue pattern

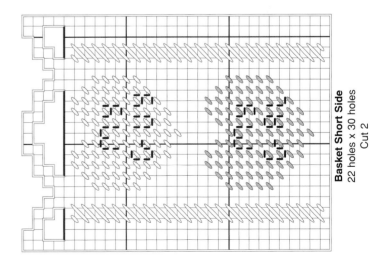

Basket Long Side
44 holes x 30 holes
Cut 2

Basket Short Side
22 holes x 30 holes
Cut 2

Basket Handle
88 holes x 9 holes
Cut 1

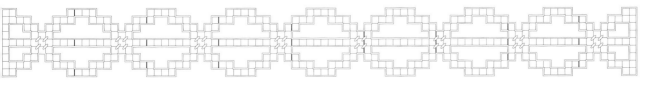

base. Following graphs, stitch bow pieces and hearts, stitching five hearts as graphed and four with white.

3. Overcast hearts and bow tails with adjacent colors. Using gold cord throughout, Overcast long edges of bow loop and bow center. Whipstitch short edges of loop together. Place seam at center back, then wrap bow center around middle of loop; Whipstitch short edges of center together.

4. Using photo as a guide, glue tails to center back of bow, then glue bow to center bottom of wreath base. Glue one red heart to center top of wreath base, then glue remaining hearts to base on both sides of center top heart, placing white hearts between red hearts.

5. Hang as desired. ❖

Metallic Heart Wreath

Design by Kimberly A. Suber

Sparkling red, white and gold metallic cord come together in this pretty keepsake wreath! Guests and family alike will love this pretty greeting.

Skill Level: Beginner

Materials

- 1 sheet 7-count plastic canvas
- 2 (6") plastic canvas radial circles
- Plastic canvas metallic cord as listed in color key
- 3 yards white plastic canvas yarn
- Hot-glue gun

Instructions

1. Cut hearts and bow pieces from plastic canvas according to graphs. Cut and keep the outermost row of holes from both circles.

2. Whipstitch outermost rows of holes on both circles together with white yarn to form wreath

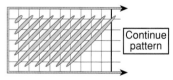

Wreath Bow Loop
50 holes x 6 holes
Cut 1

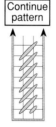

Wreath Bow Center
3 holes x 20 holes
Cut 1

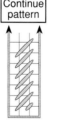

Wreath Heart
11 holes x 11 holes
Cut 9
Stitch 5 as graphed
Stitch 4 with white cord

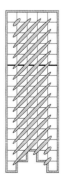

Wreath Bow Tail
5 holes x 15 holes
Cut 2

COLOR KEY	
Plastic Canvas Metallic Cord	**Yards**
■ Red	6
White	6
▢ Gold	5

Teddy Bear Cupid

Add an adorably romantic touch to your Valentine's Day outfit with this darling pin! It's quick and easy to stitch, too!

Design by Angie Arickx

COLOR KEY

Plastic Canvas Yarn	Yards
■ Red #01	3
⅛" Metallic Needlepoint Yarn	
☐ Gold #PC1	2

Color numbers given are for Uniek Needloft plastic canvas yarn and Rainbow Gallery Plastic Canvas 7 Metallic Needlepoint Yarn.

Skill Level: Beginner

Materials

- ⅛ sheet 7-count plastic canvas
- Uniek Needloft plastic canvas yarn as listed in color key
- ⅛"-wide Plastic Canvas 7 Metallic Needlepoint yarn by Rainbow Gallery as listed in color key
- #16 tapestry needle
- 1" flocked flat-backed bear
- 1" pin back
- Hot-glue gun

Instructions

1. Cut plastic canvas according to graphs.

2. Stitch pieces following graphs. Overcast wings with gold. With red, Overcast top edges of hearts from dot to dot; with wrong sides together, Whipstitch remaining edges of hearts together.

3. Glue bear inside heart and wings to back of bear above heart. Glue pin back to back of wings. ❖

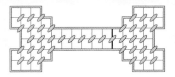

Cupid Wings
15 holes x 6 holes
Cut 1

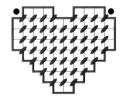

Cupid Heart
10 holes x 8 holes
Cut 2

PASTEL HEARTS

Designs by Angie Arickx

Stitch dozens of hearts as an expression of your affection on this charming three-piece set including a mug, coaster and miniature basket.

Skill Level: Beginner

Materials

- 1 sheet 10-count plastic canvas
- 4½" plastic canvas radial circle by Darice
- DMC #3 pearl cotton as listed in color key
- DMC 6-strand embroidery floss as listed in color key
- #18 tapestry needle
- White-rimmed plastic mug with insert area by Crafter's Pride

Instructions

1. Cut plastic canvas according to graphs (also see page 29).

2. Stitch pieces with pearl cotton following graphs, overlapping two holes on basket side before stitching. Continental Stitch uncoded areas with white. Radial circle will remain unstitched. Backstitch words with 6 strands ultra dark dusty rose floss over completed background stitching.

3. Overcast coaster following graph. Using white throughout, Overcast top edge of basket side and top and bottom edges of mug insert. Whipstitch short sides of insert together. Whipstitch bottom edge of basket side to radial circle.

4. Place insert inside mug, aligning seam with handle. ❖

COLOR KEY	
#3 Pearl Cotton	**Yards**
■ Light violet #554	30
■ Light aquamarine #993	20
☐ Light baby blue #3325	20
☐ Light mauve #3689	20
Uncoded areas are white Continental Stitches	18
∕ White Overcasting and Whipstitching	
6-Strand Embroidery Floss	
∕ Ultra dark dusty rose #3350 Backstitch	3
Color numbers given are for DMC #3 pearl cotton and 6-strand embroidery floss.	

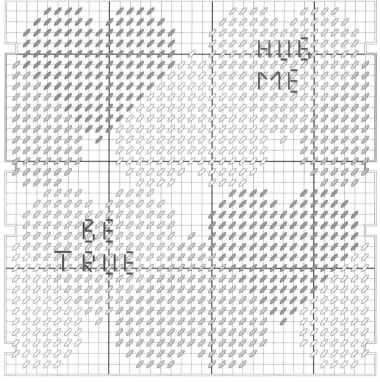

Pastel Hearts Coaster
36 holes x 35 holes
Cut 1

Continued on page 29

Hogs 'n' Kisses

Design by Vicki Blizzard

Pig collectors will be in hog heaven with this sweetheart greeting! Stitch it to share with your family or to give to a pig-loving friend!

Hyphen
3 holes x 1 hole
Cut 2

Wing
12 holes x 6 holes
Cut 4, reverse 2

Body
14 holes x 16 holes
Cut 2

Snout
4 holes x 4 holes
Stitch 2

Ear
3 holes x 3 holes
Cut 4, reverse 2

COLOR KEY	
Plastic Canvas Yarn	**Yards**
☐ White #0001	10
▨ Cherry blossom #0010	9
■ Scarlet #0022	14
■ Black #0028	1
╱ Black #0028 2-ply Straight Stitch	
Fine (#8) Braid	
╱ Gold #002HL Backstitch and Straight Stitch	4
Color numbers given are for Spinrite plastic canvas yarn and Kreinik Fine (#8) Braid.	

Skill Level: Beginner

Materials

- ½ sheet Uniek Quick-Count 7-count plastic canvas
- Uniek plastic canvas heart shape
- Spinrite plastic canvas yarn as listed in color key
- Kreinik Fine (#8) Braid as listed in color key
- #16 tapestry needle
- 4 (5mm) round black cabochons by The Beadery
- ½ yard ⅝"-wide pre-gathered gold-edged lace
- 2 yards ⅛"-wide white satin ribbon
- Sheet red felt
- Hot-glue gun

Instructions

1. Cut plastic canvas according to graphs. Using heart shape as a template, cut red felt to fit.

2. Stitch heart, wings, bodies, ears, arms and two snouts following graphs, reversing two ears and two wings before stitching. Work embroidery on snouts with 2 plies black.

3. Overcast heart, wings, bodies, ears and arms with adjacent colors. Place two unstitched snout pieces on backside of one stitched snout and Whipstitch together with cherry blossom. Repeat with remaining snout pieces.

4. Stitch and Overcast tails with cherry blossom, reversing one tail before stitching. Stitch and Overcast letters and hyphens with white, working gold braid Backstitches and Straight Stitches when stitching and Overcasting are completed.

5. Using photo as a guide through step 9, glue letters and hyphens to heart front so they read "HOGS -N- KISSES." Glue lace to back of heart around outside edge, then glue felt to back of heart.

6. Glue pig bodies to back of heart at top edges. Glue two wings to back of each pig. Glue ears, snouts and black cabochons to faces. Glue arms to front of heart and bodies. Glue tails to backs of hearts.

7. Cut two 6" lengths of ribbon. Tie each in a small bow; trim ends. Glue one bow to lower outside edge of each pig face.

8. Cut three 12" lengths of ribbon. Holding the three lengths together, tie in a bow and trim ends. Glue to bottom of heart.

9. For hanger, cut one 12" length of ribbon. Glue one end to back of each pig's head. Tie remaining ribbon in a small bow; trim ends. Glue to center of hanger. ❖

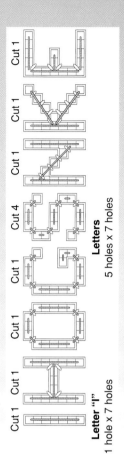

Letters
5 holes x 7 holes

Letter "I"
1 hole x 7 holes

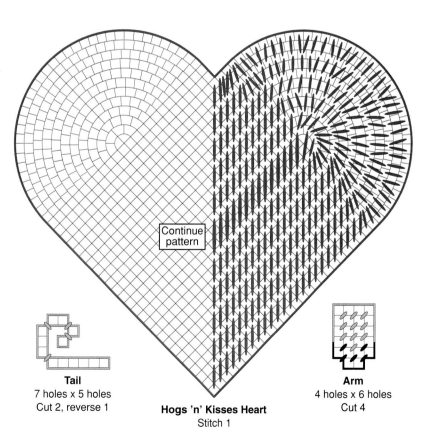

Tail
7 holes x 5 holes
Cut 2, reverse 1

Hogs 'n' Kisses Heart
Stitch 1

Arm
4 holes x 6 holes
Cut 4

Sweetheart Frame

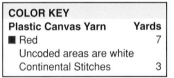

Sweetheart Frame Back
22 holes x 26 holes
Cut 1

COLOR KEY	
Plastic Canvas Yarn	**Yards**
■ Red	7
Uncoded areas are white	
Continental Stitches	3

Design by Kimberly A. Suber

Tuck a school photograph of your little sweetie in this darling red-and-white mini photo frame.

Skill Level: Beginner

Materials

- ½ sheet 7-count plastic canvas
- Plastic canvas yarn as listed in color key

Instructions

1. Cut plastic canvas according to graphs. Cut one 10-hole x 19-hole piece for frame stand.

2. Continental Stitch frame front following graph. Frame back and stand will remain unstitched.

3. Using red throughout, Overcast inside edges of frame front. Whipstitch one short edge of stand to frame back where indicated on graph with blue line. Whipstitch frame back to fame front around outside edges. ❖

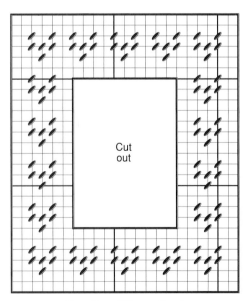

Sweetheart Frame Front
22 holes x 26 holes
Cut 1

Continued from page 25

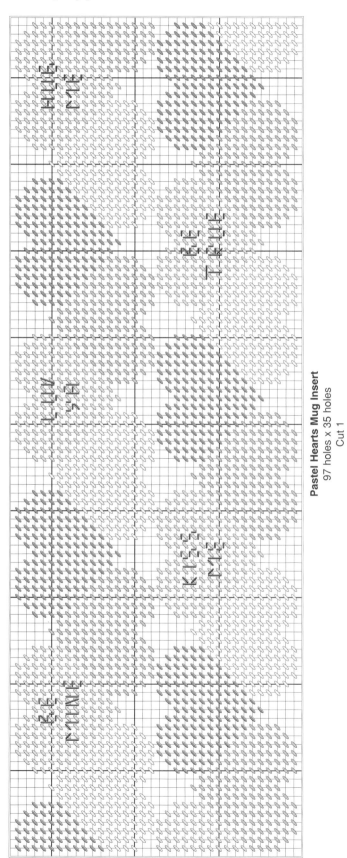

Pastel Hearts Mug Insert
97 holes x 35 holes
Cut 1

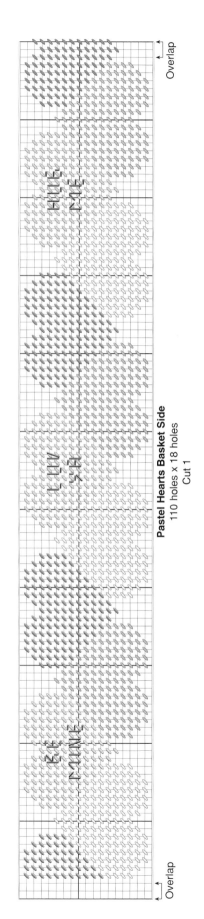

Pastel Hearts Basket Side
110 holes x 18 holes
Cut 1

St. Patrick's Day Fun

Here's a collection of cheerful and colorful projects that say, "I'm proud to be Irish!" Stitch one or all for yourself or a fun-loving Irish friend!

Bless Our Irish Home

If you're Irish, this attractive sign will help you celebrate your Irish heritage. Hang it on a door or wall to add a warm accent to your home.

Design by Vicki Blizzard • Shown on page 31

Skill Level: Beginner

Materials

- ½ sheet 7-count plastic canvas
- 6" plastic canvas radial circle
- Red Heart Classic worsted weight yarn Art. E267 as listed in color key
- Kreinik Medium (#16) Braid as listed in color key
- #16 tapestry needle
- 5" Darice Bright Jewels Metallic Cord: gold #3411-01
- 70 (3mm) round gold beads from The Beadery
- Beading needle
- Clear thread
- Sheet baby blue felt
- Hot-glue gun

Instructions

1. Cut one rainbow from plastic canvas radial circle; cut letters, one base, one pot, two clouds and 14 shamrocks from 7-count plastic canvas according to graphs (right, page 33 and page 37). Cut felt to fit base.

2. Stitch base, pot, rainbow and clouds following graphs, reversing one cloud before stitching. Overcast base and pot with adjacent colors. Overcast top edge of rainbow with amethyst and bottom edge with jockey red. Overcast clouds with white and silver following graph.

3. Overcast and stitch letters with paddy green, then work gold braid Backstitches. Overcast four shamrocks with emerald green, four with forest green and six with paddy green. Work French Knots with adjacent colors when Overcasting is completed.

4. For handle on pot, thread gold cord from front to back through holes indicated on graph, leaving ½" ends. Glue ends to backside.

5. Using photo as guide through step 6, tack handle to pot front using clear thread. Using beading needle and clear thread, attach gold beads as desired to top of pot.

6. Glue felt to wrong side of base. Glue clouds to upper corners of base, then glue rainbow to backs of clouds. Glue pot to center bottom of base, making sure bottom edges are even. Glue letters to base so they read, "BLESS OUR IRISH HOME." Glue shamrocks as desired to base front and to pot. ❖

COLOR KEY	
Worsted Weight Yarn	**Yards**
☐ White #1	4
■ Black #12	4
☐ Yellow #230	1
▨ Tangerine #253	1
▨ Silver #412	1
Emerald green #676	2
▨ Paddy green #686	11
Forest green #689	2
☐ Pale blue #815	28
▨ Olympic blue #849	1
╱ Amethyst #588 Overcasting	1
╱ Jockey red #902 Overcasting	1
● Paddy green #686 French Knot	
Medium (#16) Braid	
╱ Gold #002HL Backstitch	6
◉ Attach gold cord	
Color numbers given are for Red Heart Classic worsted weight yarn Art. E267 and Kreinik Medium (#16) Braid.	

Bless Our Irish Home Shamrock
3 holes x 3 holes
Cut 14
Stitch 6 as graphed,
4 with emerald green,
4 with forest green

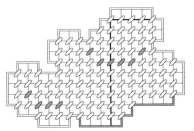

Bless Our Irish Home Cloud
17 holes x 11 holes
Cut 2, reverse 1

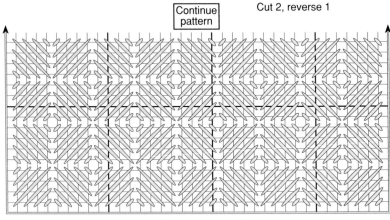

Continue pattern

Bless Our Irish Home Base
37 holes x 69 holes
Cut 1

Continued on page 37

Top o' the Mornin' Magnet

Skill Level: Beginner

Materials

- ⅛ sheet 10-count plastic canvas
- DMC #3 pearl cotton as listed in color key
- DMC #5 pearl cotton as listed in color key
- #18 tapestry needle
- 1" white flocked flat-backed bear with bow tie
- Black fabric marker
- 2" magnetic strip
- Hot-glue gun

Instructions

1. Cut plastic canvas according to graphs.

2. Continental Stitch pieces following graphs. Backstitch letters on plaque with #5 pearl cotton and buckle on hat front with #3 pearl cotton when background stitching is completed.

3. Overcast shamrock and plaque with adjacent colors. Using Christmas green throughout, Overcast bottom edges of hat front and hat back. With wrong sides together, Whipstitch hat front to hat back.

4. If bow tie on bear is not black, remove from bear and color with black fabric marker. Allow to dry. Glue bow tie in place.

5. Using photo as guide, insert right ear of bear into bottom of hat and glue in place. Glue bear to left side of plaque and shamrock to right side. Glue magnetic strip to backside of plaque. ❖

Design by Angie Arickx

Greet your Irish family with this blessing every morning by sticking this cheery magnet to the front of your refrigerator!

COLOR KEY	
#3 Pearl Cotton	**Yards**
■ Black #310	4
▨ Christmas green #909	4
Uncoded area is light Nile green #955 Continental Stitches	4
⁄ Light Nile green #955 Overcasting	
⁄ Deep canary #725 Backstitch	½
#5 Pearl Cotton	
⁄ Black #310 Backstitch	1
Color numbers given are for DMC #3 and #5 pearl cotton.	

Magnet Shamrock
13 holes x 12 holes
Cut 1

Magnet Plaque
29 holes x 9 holes
Cut 1

Magnet Hat
9 holes x 5 holes
Cut 2

Bless Our Irish Home Letters
5 holes x 7 holes

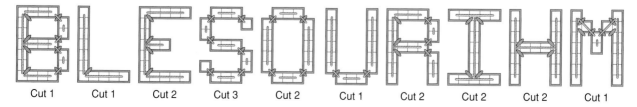

| Cut 1 | Cut 1 | Cut 2 | Cut 3 | Cut 2 | Cut 1 | Cut 2 | Cut 2 | Cut 2 | Cut 1 |

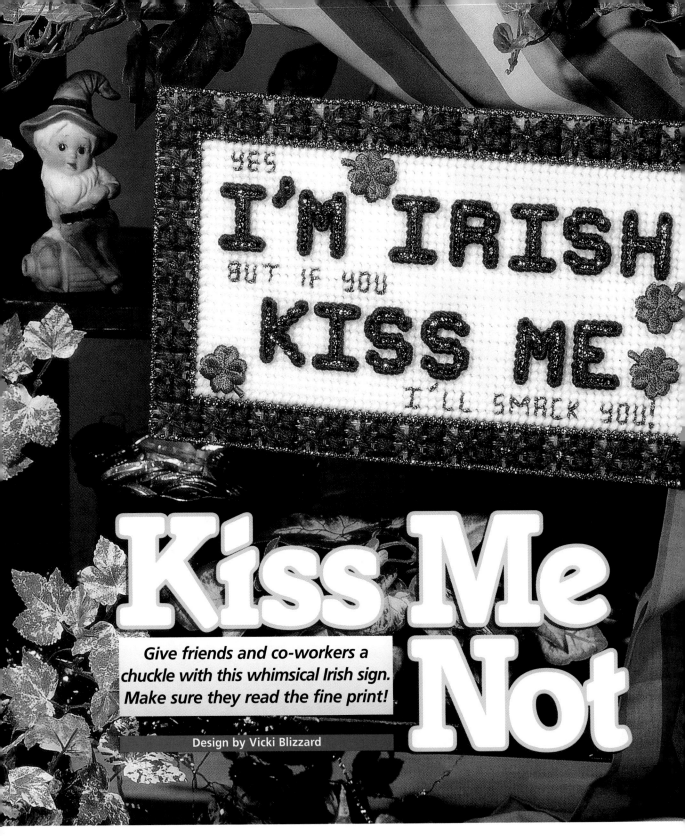

Kiss Me Not

Give friends and co-workers a chuckle with this whimsical Irish sign. Make sure they read the fine print!

Design by Vicki Blizzard

Skill Level: Beginner

Materials

- 1 sheet 7-count plastic canvas
- #16 tapestry needle
- Red Heart Classic worsted weight yarn Art. E267 as listed in color key
- ⅛"-wide Plastic Canvas 7 Metallic Needlepoint Yarn by Rainbow Gallery as listed in color key
- ¹⁄₁₆"-wide Plastic Canvas 10 Metallic Needlepoint Yarn by Rainbow Gallery as listed in color key
- 4 shamrock appliqués
- Sheet white felt
- Sawtooth hanger
- Hot-glue gun

Instructions

1. Cut plastic canvas according to graphs. Cut felt to fit back of sign.

2. Stitch paddy green border on sign following graph and Fig. 1. Continental Stitch center of sign with ⅛"-wide copper yarn and white yarn following graph. Overcast with ⅛"-wide copper yarn. Work embroidery with ¹⁄₁₆"-wide copper yarn over completed background stitching.

3. Stitch and Overcast letters with paddy green yarn following graphs, then work embroidery on letters with ¹⁄₁₆"-wide copper yarn.

4. Using photo as a guide, glue letters on sign to read "I'M IRISH KISS ME." Glue shamrocks to sign. Glue felt to backside of sign. Glue sawtooth hanger to center top backside of sign. ❖

COLOR KEY	
Worsted Weight Yarn	**Yards**
☐ White #1	23
▨ Paddy green #686	14
⅛" Metallic Needlepoint Yarn	
▨ Copper #PC3	6
¹⁄₁₆" Metallic Needlepoint Yarn	
⁄ Copper #PM53 Backstitch and Straight Stitch	5
⦿ Copper #PM53 French Knot	
Color numbers given are for Red Heart Classic worsted weight yarn Art. E267 and Rainbow Gallery Plastic Canvas 7 Needlepoint Yarn and Plastic Canvas 10 Needlepoint Yarn.	

Fig. 1

Bring needle up
at 1, down at 2,
up at 3, down
at 4, etc.

Apostrophe
2 holes x 3 holes
Cut 1

Letters
5 holes x 7 holes

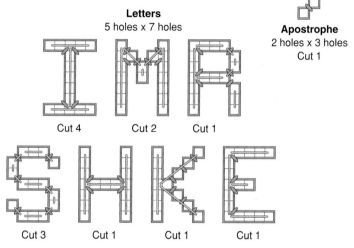

Cut 4   Cut 2   Cut 1

Cut 3   Cut 1   Cut 1   Cut 1

Kiss Me Not Sign
71 holes x 41 holes
Cut 1

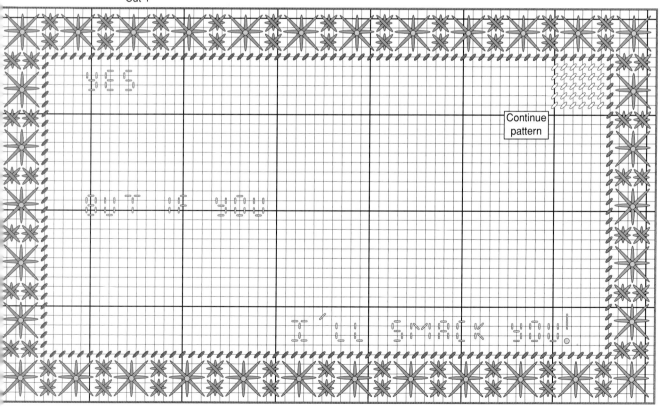

Continue pattern

Bless the Irish

Design by Carol Nartowicz

This green-and-white door hanger pays tribute to all Irish men and women, and bestows a blessing on them one and all!

Skill Level: Beginner

Materials
- 1 sheet 7-count white plastic canvas
- Small amount 7-count clear plastic canvas
- Uniek Needloft plastic canvas yarn as listed in color key
- Uniek Needloft metallic craft cord as listed in color key
- Fusible fleece
- Hot-glue gun

Instructions

1. Cut two door hangers from white plastic canvas; cut one hat and one buckle from clear plastic canvas according to graphs. Cut fusible fleece to fit hanger. Hanger back and buckle will remain unstitched.

2. Stitch hat following graph; Overcast with Christmas green. Wrap gold cord around buckle. Place fusible fleece on backside of sign front, then stitch front through fleece following graph.

3. Whipstitch back to front with white. Using photo as a guide, glue buckle to right side of hat, then glue hat at an angle to left side of sign under doorknob opening. ❖

COLOR KEY	
Plastic Canvas Yarn	**Yards**
☐ Christmas green #28	8
■ Forest #29	4
∕ White #41 Whipstitching	5
Metallic Craft Cord	
☐ Gold #01	1
Color numbers given are for Uniek Needloft plastic canvas yarn and metallic craft cord.	

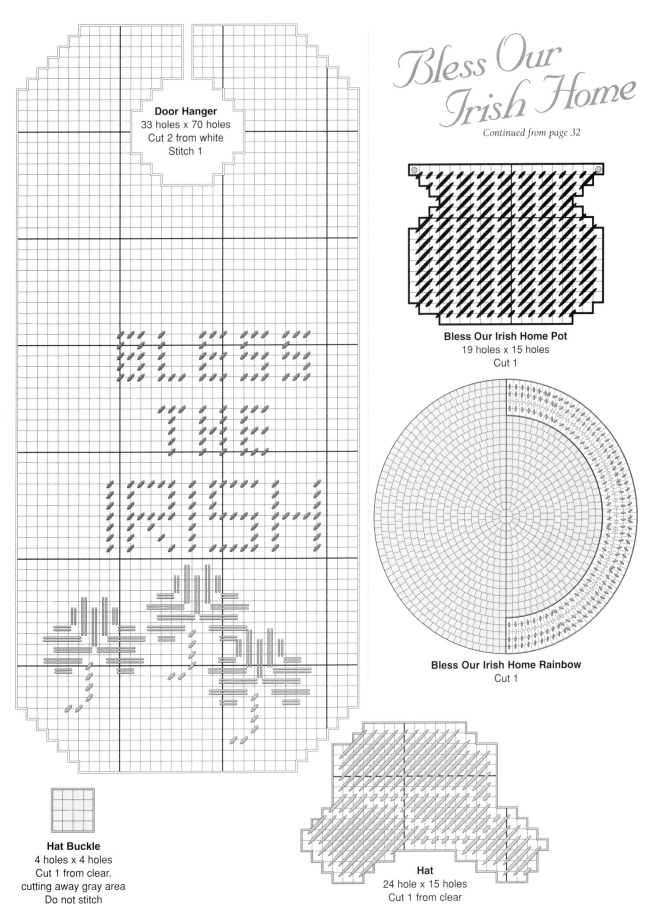

Door Hanger
33 holes x 70 holes
Cut 2 from white
Stitch 1

Bless Our Irish Home
Continued from page 32

Bless Our Irish Home Pot
19 holes x 15 holes
Cut 1

Bless Our Irish Home Rainbow
Cut 1

Hat Buckle
4 holes x 4 holes
Cut 1 from clear,
cutting away gray area
Do not stitch

Hat
24 hole x 15 holes
Cut 1 from clear

Irish Party Favors

Pot o' Gold Favor

Design by Celia Lange Designs

Skill Level: Beginner

Materials

- ⅓ sheet 7-count plastic canvas
- Red Heart Super Saver worsted weight yarn Art. E301 as listed in color key
- ¼ yard ⅛"-wide green satin ribbon
- Gold candy or chocolate coins
- Low-temperature glue gun

Instructions

1. Cut plastic canvas according to graphs.

2. Stitch pieces following graphs. Overcast clover with spring green. Using black throughout, Overcast handles. Whipstitch pot sides together, alternating sides A and B. Overcast top and bottom edges of pot.

3. Glue handles to opposite sides of pot. Center and glue pot to clover. Tie ribbon in a small bow, trimming ends; glue to pot at one handle end.

4. Fill pot with candy. ❖

Invite your friends to a St. Patrick's Day brunch and delight them with these fun-to-make party favors!

Favor Handle
9 holes x 2 holes
Cut 2

COLOR KEY

Worsted Weight Yarn	Yards
■ Black #312	5
▨ Spring green #367	3

Color numbers given are for Red Heart Super Saver worsted weight yarn Art. E301.

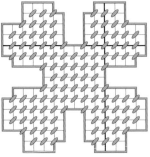

Favor Clover
14 holes x 14 holes
Cut 1

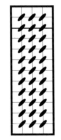

Favor Side B
4 holes x 12 holes
Cut 4

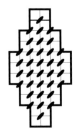

Favor Side A
6 holes x 11 holes
Cut 4

Leprechaun Pin

Design by Vicki Blizzard

Skill Level: Beginner

Materials

- Small amount 10-count plastic canvas
- DMC #3 pearl cotton as listed in color key
- DMC 6-strand embroidery floss as listed in color key
- Kreinik Medium (#16) Braid as listed in color key
- #22 tapestry needle
- 2 (4mm) black cabochons by The Beadery
- Small amount rust Bumples doll hair by One & Only Creations
- 2 (7mm) gold jump rings
- 1" gold pin back
- Jewelry pliers
- Hot-glue gun

Instructions

1. Cut plastic canvas according to graphs.

2. Stitch pieces following graphs, reversing one shoe before stitching. Overcast face, hands and hat with adjacent colors. Overcast shoes with black, socks with Christmas green and base with green braid.

3. Work French Knot on nose, wrapping pearl cotton around needle two times. Using 6 strands floss, work Backstitches on face for mouth and Straight Stitches on hands for fingers. Work buckle on hat and laces on shoes with gold braid. Work letters on base with green braid.

4. Using photo as a guide through step 6, glue cabochons to face for eyes. For beard, wrap doll hair four times around two fingers. Slide loops of fingers and tie in center with a 4" strand of doll hair, forming a bundle. Glue bundle to chin. Repeat four more times, gluing two bundles to face on each side of chin bundle. Trim beard to ½".

5. Open jump rings with pliers and attach to base, then attach one jump ring to each shoe where indicated with blue dots on graphs; close rings.

6. Glue hat to head at an angle. Glue head to top part of base, then glue one hand to each side of base. Glue pin back to backside of base. ❖

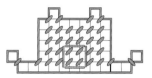

Leprechaun Pin Hat
13 holes x 6 holes
Cut 1

Leprechaun Pin Hand
5 holes x 4 holes
Cut 2

Leprechaun Pin Shoe
7 holes x 7 holes
Cut 2, reverse 1

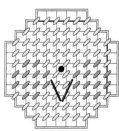

Leprechaun Pin Face
11 holes x 11 holes
Cut 1

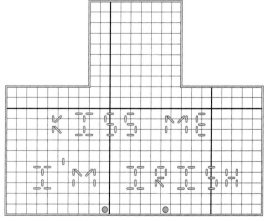

Leprechaun Pin Base
25 holes x 20 holes
Cut 1

Happy Easter

Elegant inspirational designs as well as whimsical Easter projects will make your Easter celebrations extra-special and extra-colorful! Attractive crosses, sparkling Easter eggs, charming tissue box covers and more will add a lovely decorating touch to your home throughout the spring season!

Nothing says "Spring has sprung!" quite like the appearance of beautiful and bold tulips! Stitch this charming centerpiece basket and favor set to welcome spring into your home!

Skill Level: Beginner

Materials
Both Projects
- Red Heart Classic worsted weight yarn Art. E267 as listed in color key
- #16 tapestry needle
- Hot-glue gun

Tulip Basket
- 2 sheets 7-count plastic canvas
- Darice 6" plastic canvas radial circle
- Felt:
  2 sheets shocking pink
  ¼ yard kelly green

Each Tulip Cup
- ¼ sheet 7-count plastic canvas
- Darice 3" plastic canvas radial circle
- 3½" square kelly green felt

Project Note
Instructions are given for one tulip cup only. Use colors desired for each cup side; color for cup bottom is the same for each cup. Samples also used yellow #230, medium coral #252 and jockey red #902 for cup sides.

Tulip Basket
1. Cut six petals and two leaf handles from plastic canvas according to graphs. Using pattern given (see page 44), cut lining for six petal sides from shocking pink felt. Using plastic canvas leaf as a template, cut two leaf handles from kelly green felt. On kelly green felt, trace around 6" circle. Cut felt circle, then trim ⅛" off outside edge.

2. Stitch leaf handles following graph. Overcast outside edges with paddy green. Glue felt handle to back of each stitched handle. Allow to dry. Trim edges as needed. With wrong sides together, Whipstitch dart of each handle together.

3. Stitch basket bottom following graph. Using paddy green through step 4, Overcast outside edge of basket bottom with paddy green.

4. With wrong side of handle facing right side of basket bottom, Whipstitch bottom edge of one handle to one edge indicated on basket bottom graph. Whipstitch remaining handle to edge indicated on opposite side of basket bottom graph. Glue felt circle to wrong side of basket bottom. To join handles, tack tips of handle pieces together.

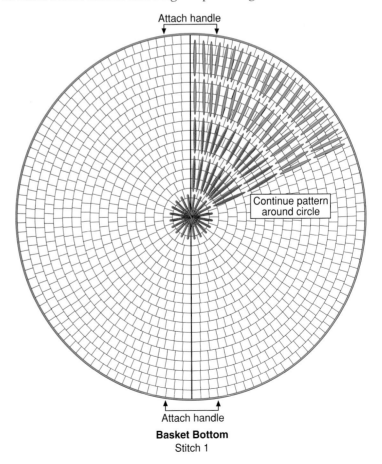

Attach handle

Continue pattern around circle

Attach handle

Basket Bottom
Stitch 1

Time

5. Using grenadine throughout, stitch and Overcast each petal side following graph. With right sides together, Whipstitch dart of each petal together. Whipstitch wrong sides of two petals together from blue dot to blue dot. Whipstitch all petals together in this manner, Whip-stitching first and last petals together to close basket sides. Overcast

top and bottom edges.

6. Glue one felt petal to back of each stitched petal. Center and glue bottom of petals to top of basket bottom. Glue bottom section of each leaf to basket.

Tulip Cup

1. Cut one cup side from plastic canvas according to graph (page 44). On kelly green felt, trace around 3" circle. Cut felt circle, then trim ⅛" off outside edge.

2. Stitch cup bottom following graph; Overcast with paddy green. Glue felt to wrong side of cup bottom.

3. Using grenadine throughout, stitch cup side between blue dots following graph. Overlap one hole as indicated on graph and stitch remainder of side. Whipstitch each bottom dart together; Overcast top and bottom edges.

4. Center and glue bottom of side to top of basket bottom. ❖

COLOR KEY
TULIP BASKET

Worsted Weight Yarn	Yards
■ Paddy green #686	34
■ Grenadine #730	49
╱ Grenadine #730 Straight Stitch	

Color numbers given are for Red Heart Classic worsted weight yarn Art. E267.

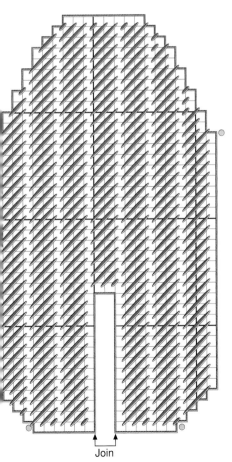

Basket Petal Side
22 holes x 39 holes
Cut 6

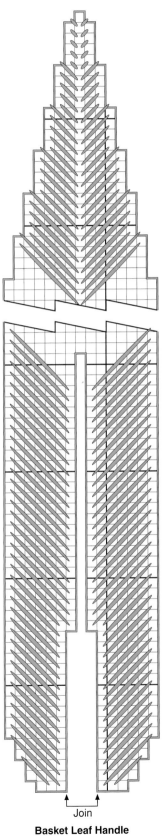

Basket Leaf Handle
15 holes x 90 holes
Cut 2

COLOR KEY
TULIP CUP

Worsted Weight Yarn	Yards
■ Grenadine #730	8
■ Paddy green #686	3

Color numbers given are for Red Heart
Classic worsted weight yarn Art. E267.

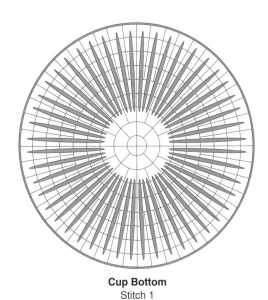

Cup Bottom
Stitch 1

Basket Petal Side Lining
Cut 6 from
shocking pink felt

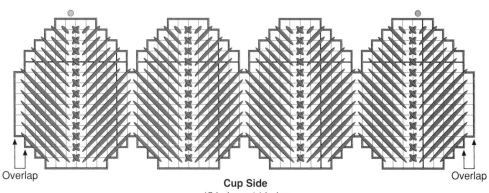

Overlap

Overlap

Cup Side
45 holes x 14 holes
Cut 1

4. If felt backing is desired, cut felt to fit bunny. Glue to back of bunny and ribbon. ❖

backside of bunny behind ears. Allow to dry thoroughly. Apply seam sealant to ribbon ends.

Bunny Bookmark

Design by Judi Kauffman

This little darling makes a delightful bookmark for your Bible or any favorite book. Readers of all ages will appreciate this as a thoughtful gift!

Skill Level: Beginner

Materials

- Small amount 14-count plastic canvas
- Anchor 6-strand embroidery floss as listed in color key
- 10" Kreinik ⅛" Ribbon: amethyst #026
- 6 small purple flowers
- 9" 1"-wide purple grosgrain ribbon
- Seam sealant
- Small amount off-white felt (optional)
- Tacky glue

Instructions

1. Cut plastic canvas according to graph.

2. Following graph, Continental Stitch bunny with 6 strands floss. Work French Knot nose with 6 strands light carnation. Using dark antique blue, Straight Stitch whiskers with 1 strand, Backstitch between ears with 2 strands and work French Knot eyes with 6 strands. Edges are not Overcast.

3. Using photo as a guide, gather flowers in a bouquet and glue to bunny under nose. Tie amethyst ribbon in a bow and glue under flowers. Glue grosgrain ribbon to

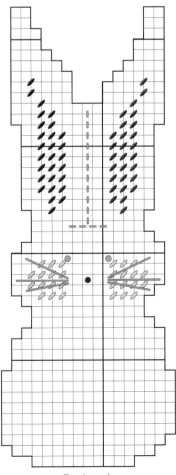

Bookmark
17 holes x 43 holes
Cut 1

Decorative Easter Eggs

Designs by Angie Arickx

Create this pair of Fabergé-like eggs to cherish and display year after year! Sparkling metallics and pretty pearl cotton make these lovely designs keepsake-quality!

Skill Level: Intermediate

Materials

- ½ sheet 10-count plastic canvas
- DMC #3 pearl cotton as listed in color key
- ¹⁄₁₆"-wide Plastic Canvas 10 Metallic Needlepoint Yarn by Rainbow Gallery as listed in color key
- #18 tapestry needle
- Tacky glue

Instructions

1. For each egg, cut one egg, one ring base, one large cap and two small caps from plastic canvas according to graphs.

2. Stitch pieces following graphs, overlapping egg and base pieces before stitching. Work Backstitches and French Knots on eggs over completed background stitching.

3. Using matching metallic needlepoint yarn throughout, Overcast caps and bases. Whipstitch darts on each egg together, joining sections.

4. Glue one corresponding small cap to bottom of each egg. Glue one corresponding large cap to top of each egg, then center and glue remaining small cap to top of large cap.

5. Place eggs into corresponding bases. ❖

Overlap   Overlap

Gold Egg Ring Base
Silver Egg Ring Base
40 holes x 4 holes
Cut 1 for each egg

Gold Egg Small Cap
Silver Egg Small Cap
4 holes x 4 holes
Cut 2 for each egg

Gold Egg Large Cap
Silver Egg Large Cap
6 holes x 6 holes
Cut 1 for each egg

COLOR KEY	
SILVER EASTER EGG	
#3 Pearl Cotton	**Yards**
☐ Light pistachio green #368	1
☐ Medium pink #776	1
■ Medium rose #899	1
Uncoded areas are white Continental Stitches	12
✎ Light pistachio green #368 Backstitch	
¹⁄₁₆" Metallic Needlepoint Yarn	
☐ Silver #PM 52	10
○ Silver #PM 52 French Knot	
Color numbers given are for DMC #3 pearl cotton and Rainbow Gallery Plastic Canvas 10 Metallic Needlepoint Yarn.	

COLOR KEY	
GOLD EASTER EGG	
#3 Pearl Cotton	**Yards**
■ Medium lavender #208	1
☐ Light lavender #210	1
☐ Blue green #502	1
Uncoded areas are cream #746 Continental Stitches	12
✎ Blue green #502 Backstitch	
¹⁄₁₆" Metallic Needlepoint Yarn	
☐ Gold #PM 51	10
○ Gold #PM 51 French Knot	
Color numbers given are for DMC #3 pearl cotton and Rainbow Gallery Plastic Canvas 10 Metallic Needlepoint Yarn.	

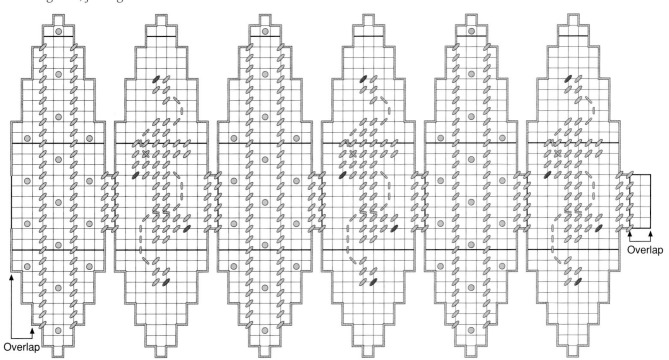

Overlap

Overlap

Gold Egg & Silver Egg
62 holes x 32 holes
Cut 1 for each egg

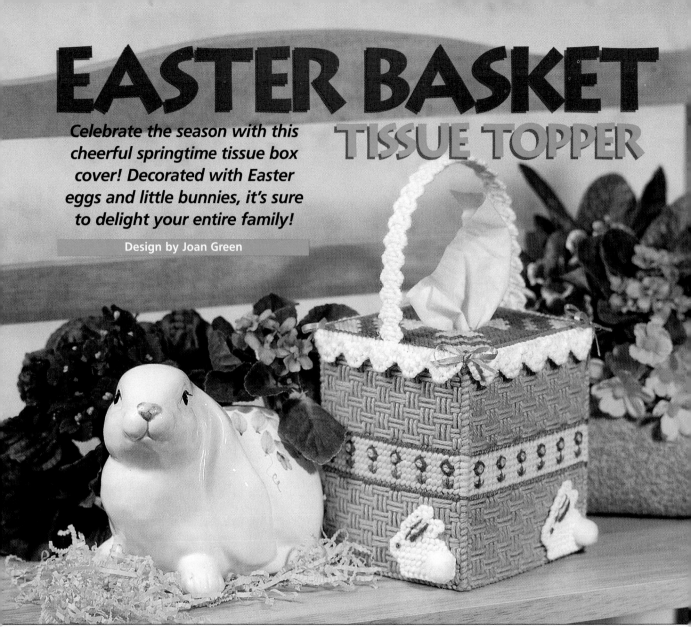

EASTER BASKET
TISSUE TOPPER

Celebrate the season with this cheerful springtime tissue box cover! Decorated with Easter eggs and little bunnies, it's sure to delight your entire family!

Design by Joan Green

Skill Level: Intermediate

Materials

- 1⅔ sheets 7-count plastic canvas
- Spinrite Bernat Berella "4" worsted weight yarn as listed in color key
- Spinrite plastic canvas yarn as listed in color key
- #16 tapestry needle
- 32" ⅛"-wide peach satin ribbon
- 4 (½") white pompoms
- Hot-glue gun

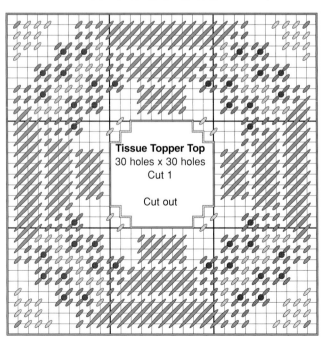

Tissue Topper Top
30 holes x 30 holes
Cut 1

Cut out

Instructions

1. Cut plastic canvas according to graphs.

2. Stitch pieces following graphs, working uncoded areas on sides and top with baby yellow Continental Stitches. Overcast inside edges on top with adjacent colors while stitching. Overcast bunnies, lace trim pieces and handle with white while stitching.

3. Work embroidery on sides and lace trim with 4 plies yarn. Work French Knots on top with 2 plies yarn. Use 2 plies dark Oxford heather and 4 plies arbutus for embroidery on bunnies.

4. Whipstitch sides together with adjacent colors; Whipstitch sides to top with medium lagoon. Overcast bottom edges of sides with light lagoon.

5. Using photo as a guide through step 6, with white yarn, tack handle ends to opposite sides of topper. Glue lace trim to top edges of sides, placing trim over handles on two sides.

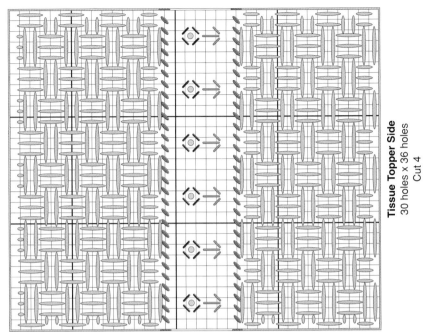

Tissue Topper Side
30 holes x 36 holes
Cut 4

Glue bunnies to bottom right side on sides, making sure bottom edges are even. Glue pompoms to bunnies for tails.

6. Cut peach ribbon into four 8" lengths. Tie each length in a bow, trimming ends as desired. Glue one bow to each top corner of topper. ❖

Tissue Topper Handle
53 holes x 53 holes
Cut 1

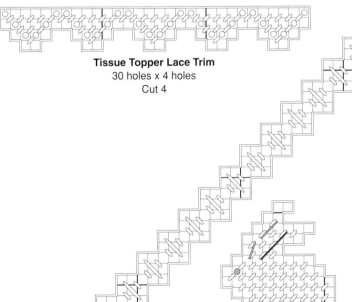

Tissue Topper Lace Trim
30 holes x 4 holes
Cut 4

Tissue Topper Bunny
11 holes x 11 holes
Cut 4

COLOR KEY	
Worsted Weight Yarn	**Yards**
▨ Light lagoon #8820	46
▦ Medium lagoon #8821	8
☐ White #8942	26
Uncoded areas are baby yellow #8945 Continental Stitches	16
⁄ Baby yellow #8945 Whipstitching	
⁄ Medium lagoon #8821 Backstitch	
⁄ Dark Oxford heather #8893 Backstitch	1
⁄ Arbutus #8922 Backstitch and Straight Stitch	4
● Dark Oxford heather #8893 French Knot	
● Arbutus #8922 French Knot	
○ White #8942 French Knot	
Plastic Canvas Yarn	
▨ Peach #0007	4
▩ Lilac #0008	10
● Peach #0007 French Knot	
Color numbers given are for Spinrite Bernat Berella "4" worsted weight yarn and Spinrite plastic canvas yarn.	

Devotional Cross

Design by Vicki Blizzard

Vibrant violets adorned with gold beads add elegance and beauty to th[is] inspirational project. Hang it all year-round as a quie[t] reminder of your faith.

Skill Level: Beginner

Materials

- 2 artist-size sheets Uniek Quick-Count stiff 7-count plastic canvas
- 1 regular-size sheet Uniek Quick-Count 7-count plastic canvas
- Red Heart Classic worsted weight yarn Art. E267 as listed in color key
- Darice Bright Jewels Metallic Cord as listed in color key
- #16 tapestry needle
- 55 (3mm) round gold beads from The Beadery
- Sewing needle and clear thread
- Sawtooth hanger
- Hot-glue gun

Instructions

1. Cut plastic canvas according to graphs (right and page 57). Cross back will remain unstitched.

2. Stitch pieces following graphs. Using gold throughout, Overcast letters and banner. Whipstitch cross front to cross back.

3. Overcast leaves with forest green and flowers with purple. Attach gold beads where indicated on flowers with sewing needle and clear thread.

4. Glue sawtooth hanger to center top backside of cross.

5. Using photo as a guide, glue letters to banner so they spell "THY WILL BE DONE." Center and glue banner on crossbar. Glue two leaves at banner top, three at bottom and one on each side; glue three large flowers at top, three at bottom and two on each side. Glue small flowers in a circle to top of cross. ❖

Cross Letters

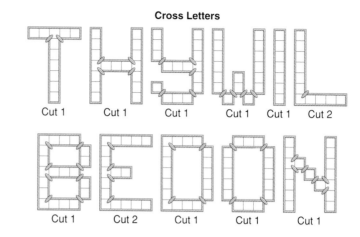

Cut 1   Cut 1   Cut 1   Cut 1   Cut 1   Cut 2

Cut 1   Cut 2   Cut 1   Cut 1   Cut 1

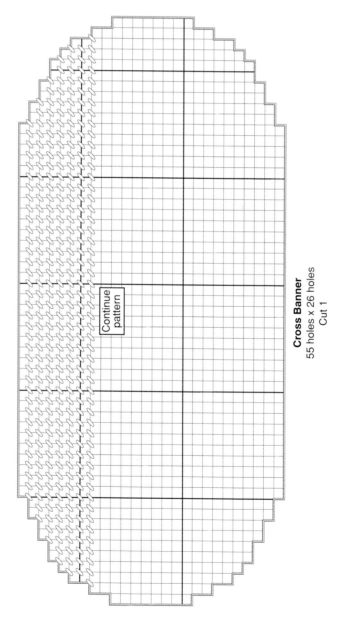

Continue pattern

Cross Banner
55 holes x 26 holes
Cut 1

Graphs continued on page 57

Easter Cross Ornaments

Designs by Angie Arickx

Quick and easy to stitch, this set of four ornaments is just right for hanging in a window or on your car's rearview mirror.

Skill Level: Beginner

Materials

- ½ sheet 7-count plastic canvas
- Uniek Needloft plastic canvas yarn as listed in color key
- Darice Bright Pearls pearlized metallic cord as listed in color key
- #16 tapestry needle

Instructions

1. Cut plastic canvas according to graphs.

2. Stitch crosses with yarn and pearlized cord following graphs. Work embroidery over completed background stitching and Overcast edges with pearlized cord.

Fig. 1
Lark's Head Knot

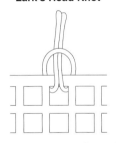

3. Cut a 10" length of pearlized cord for each cross. Work a Lark's Head Knot (Fig. 1) in holes indicated on graphs; tie ends in a knot. ❖

Aqua Cross
19 holes x 33 holes
Cut 1

Blue Cross
19 holes x 33 holes
Cut 1

Lilac Cross
19 holes x 33 holes
Cut 1

Pink Cross
19 holes x 33 holes
Cut 1

TULIP
Garden

Design by Vicki Blizzard

Delight your family at this year's Easter brunch with this pretty table centerpiece. Fill the tulip cups with colorful eggs or special Easter treats!

Skill Level: Intermediate

Materials

- 1 sheet Uniek Quick-Count 7-count stiff plastic canvas
- 3 sheets Uniek Quick-Count 7-count regular plastic canvas
- Uniek Needloft plastic canvas yarn as listed in color key
- #16 tapestry needle
- 1 yard ¾"-wide white eyelet
- Hot-glue gun

Instructions

1. Cut stems from stiff plastic canvas and remaining pieces from regular plastic canvas according to graphs (also see page 56). From regular plastic canvas, also cut four 40-hole x 25-hole pieces for inside supports and one 70-hole x 34-hole piece for garden bottom. Inside supports and bottom will remain unstitched.

2. Using watermelon and following graph, stitch three tulips, overlapping one hole where indicated before stitching; Whipstitch bottom darts closed, then Overcast top and bottom edges. Repeat with remaining three tulips, replacing watermelon with yellow.

3. Following graphs, stitch stem pieces, leaves and garden top, leaving bottom 22 bars of each stem piece unstitched.

4. Using fern throughout, Overcast inside and outside edges of top. With wrong sides together, Whipstitch dart at bottom of each leaf together, then Overcast remaining edges. Whipstitch long edges of corresponding stem pieces together; Overcast top and bottom edges.

5. Glue one watermelon tulip to end of one medium stem. Glue one yellow tulip to top of each long stem. Glue remaining flowers to tops of short stems.

6. Stitch garden sides following graphs. Using yellow throughout, Whipstitch sides together, then Whipstitch sides to bottom. Overcast top edges. Glue eyelet along inside top edge of garden sides so that about ½" shows at top.

7. Roll one support piece into a cylinder, overlapping short edges one hole; Whipstitch together with fern. Repeat for remaining three support pieces.

8. On wrong side of garden top, glue support pieces at corners around each opening. Turn right side up and place top inside garden. Glue outside edges of garden top to inside edges of garden sides.

9. Using photo as a guide, place a line of glue around bottom edge of stems, placing small stems in holes in front row, medium stem in center hole of back row and large stems in end holes of back row. Press firmly in place on garden bottom until glue sets. Glue two leaves to each stem at garden top. ❖

Graphs continued on next page

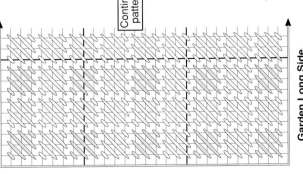

Continue pattern

Garden Long Side
70 holes x 28 holes
Cut 2 from regular
Garden Short Side
34 holes x 28 holes
Cut 2 from regular

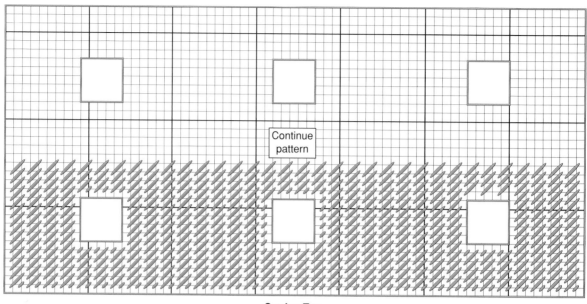

Garden Top
69 holes x 33 holes
Cut 1 from regular

COLOR KEY

Plastic Canvas Yarn	Yards
☐ Straw #19	45
▨ Fern #23	136
☐ White #41	17
▨ Watermelon #55	22
▨ Yellow #57	47

Color numbers given are for Uniek Needloft plastic canvas yarn.

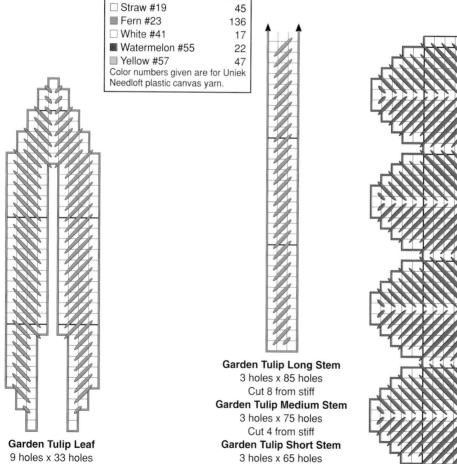

Garden Tulip Leaf
9 holes x 33 holes
Cut 12 from regular

Garden Tulip Long Stem
3 holes x 85 holes
Cut 8 from stiff

Garden Tulip Medium Stem
3 holes x 75 holes
Cut 4 from stiff

Garden Tulip Short Stem
3 holes x 65 holes
Cut 12 from stiff

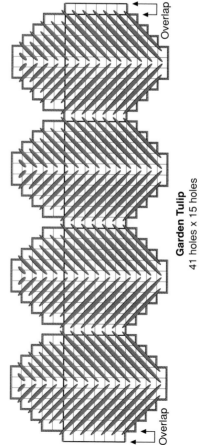

Garden Tulip
41 holes x 15 holes
Cut 6 from regular
Stitch 3 as graphed
Stitch 3 with yellow

Devotional Cross

Continued from page 51

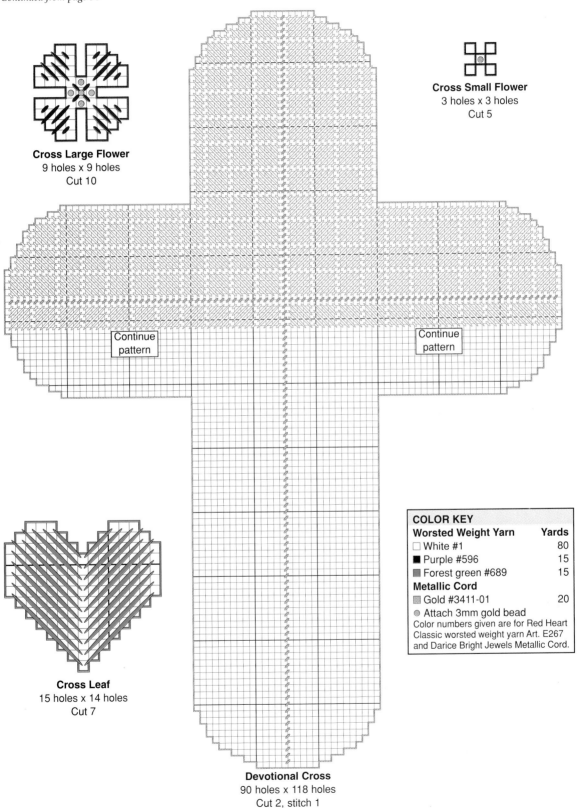

Cross Large Flower
9 holes x 9 holes
Cut 10

Cross Small Flower
3 holes x 3 holes
Cut 5

Continue pattern

Continue pattern

Cross Leaf
15 holes x 14 holes
Cut 7

COLOR KEY	
Worsted Weight Yarn	**Yards**
☐ White #1	80
■ Purple #596	15
▨ Forest green #689	15
Metallic Cord	
▨ Gold #3411-01	20
● Attach 3mm gold bead	

Color numbers given are for Red Heart Classic worsted weight yarn Art. E267 and Darice Bright Jewels Metallic Cord.

Devotional Cross
90 holes x 118 holes
Cut 2, stitch 1

Spring VEGGIES

Design by Judi Kauffman

Stitched with paper raffia and dressed up with vegetables and flowers, this basket, napkin ring and notepad holder makes a great kitchen accent during spring and summer.

Skill Level: Intermediate

Materials

- 1 sheet 7-count plastic canvas
- 2 (7¼"-diameter) ¼" foam core board circles
- Bucilla Raffia Point paper raffia as listed in color key
- #16 tapestry needle
- 10 (4"-long) artificial carrots
- 1¼" silk flower
- 3¾"–4¼"-long artificial pea pod
- 3" x 5" notepad
- 2 (3½" x 2") magnet strips
- Black felt for lining and backing
- Tacky glue

Project Notes

When working with paper raffia, use ¾–1-yard lengths for easier handling.

Push or pull needle straight up and straight down through holes while stitching with paper raffia.

Keep paper raffia smooth and flat. To prevent twisting, guide between thumb and forefinger of free hand. Drop needle occasionally and smooth with fingers to untwist.

If a mistake is made, unthread needle and use eye end of needle to loosen and remove stitches.

Fabric may be substituted for lining and backing. Cut pieces large enough to fold raw edges under.

Instructions

1. Cut plastic canvas according to graphs (page 60).

2. Following graphs and Fig. 1, stitch basket sides and notepad holder. Before stitching, join two basket sides together by overlapping two holes at both short edges, forming a circle. Overcast notepad holder and top and bottom edges of basket side, alternating medium lavender with citron.

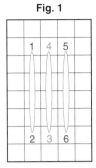

Fig. 1

Bring needle up at 1, down at 2, up at 3, down at 4, etc.

3. Work center stitches with golden natural on napkin ring following graph and Fig. 1, overlapping two holes on short edges as indicated. Stitch over top and bottom edges with brown as indicated on graph.

4. Cut felt to fit inside napkin ring and basket sides and to fit backside of notepad holder; glue in place.

5. Cut two pieces felt to fit 7¼" circles. Glue foam core board circles together, forming base. Place book on top to prevent warping. Allow to dry. Glue felt circles to top and bottom of base. Making sure bottom edges are even, glue bottom of basket side to edge of base, using a small amount of glue to prevent seepage.

6. Using photo as a guide through step 7, evenly space and glue carrots to basket sides. Cut three or four 1½"–2" strips each of medium lavender and citron paper raffia. Glue flower and paper raffia strips to napkin ring.

7. Glue pea pod just above golden natural stitches at top of notepad holder. If desired, use matching thread to tack vine tendril in place on front side of holder. ❖

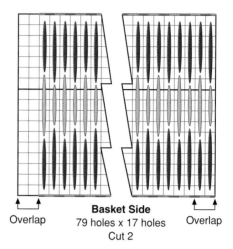

COLOR KEY

Paper Raffia	Yards
▨ Golden natural #27038	40
◼ Brown #27039	40
⟋ Medium lavender #27027 Overcasting	8
⟋ Citron #27052 Overcasting	8

Color numbers given are for Bucilla Raffia Point paper raffia.

Overlap

Basket Side
79 holes x 17 holes
Cut 2

Overlap

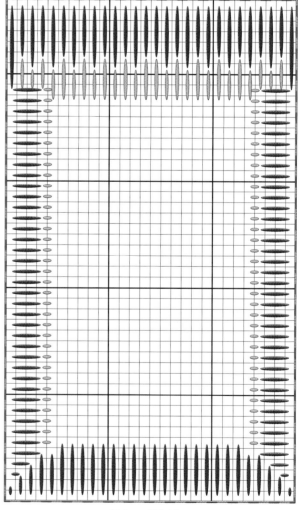

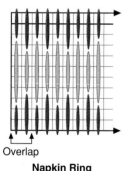

Overlap

Napkin Ring
41 holes x 11 holes
Cut 1

Notepad Holder
28 holes x 47 holes
Cut 1

Just for Mom & DAD

Stitch thoughtful gifts for your parents this Mother's Day and Father's Day, and watch their faces light up! A handsome Southwest desk set will please Dad, while a sweet pocket nosegay is sure to delight Mom. These projects and more will be cherished forever.

MOTHER'S SAMPLER

Design by Celia Lange Designs

Show your mother how special she is by stitching just a few of her most loving attributes on this keepsake sampler. She'll cherish the gift, and your expression of love.

What Is a Mother?

a warm smile

a caring hug

a loving heart

Skill Level: Intermediate

Materials

- 1 sheet 7-count plastic canvas
- Red Heart Super Saver worsted weight yarn Art. E301 as listed in color key
- DMC #3 pearl cotton as listed in color key
- ⅓ yard ⅜"-wide light pink picot-edge satin ribbon
- Sheet pink Fun Foam craft foam by Westrim Crafts
- Cardboard
- Low-temperature glue gun

Instructions

1. Cut plastic canvas.

2. Stitch background. When background stitching is completed, Backstitch letters with bright Christmas green pearl cotton. For border, couch raspberry Straight Stitches with medium delft pearl cotton. Overcast with pink.

3. Cut cardboard slightly smaller than stitched piece. Using photo as guide, glue ribbon ends to top back of sampler. Glue cardboard to back of sampler, covering ribbon ends. Cut craft foam to cover cardboard; glue in place. ❖

COLOR KEY	
Worsted Weight Yarn	**Yards**
☐ White #311	27
☐ Bright yellow #324	3
▨ Light periwinkle #347	5
☐ Spring green #367	9
▨ Paddy green #368	7
☐ Pink #371	30
■ Raspberry #375	5
╱ Raspberry #375 Straight Stitch	
#3 Pearl Cotton	
╱ Bright Christmas green #700 Backstitch	6 2
╱ Medium delft #799 Couching Stitch	
● Bright Christmas green #700 French Knot	

Color numbers given are for Red Heart Super Saver worsted weight yarn Art. E301 and DMC #3 pearl cotton.

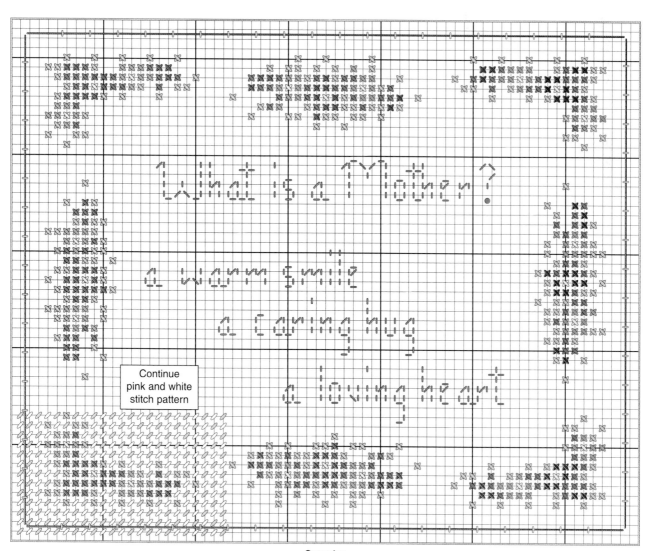

Continue pink and white stitch pattern

Sampler
68 holes x 54 holes
Cut 1

Floral Nosegay

Design by Kathleen Marie O'Donnell

Every woman loves to receive flowers, and with this pretty project, you'll give Mom flowers she can enjoy all year-round!

Skill Level: Beginner

Materials

- ½ sheet 7-count plastic canvas
- DMC #3 pearl cotton as listed in color key
- DMC 6-strand divisible metallic floss as listed in color key
- Large-eye tapestry needle
- 14" mediumweight ivory cord
- 3–4 stems assorted small silk or dried flowers
- 3 size 8/0 yellow glass beads
- Needle and off-white sewing thread
- Sheet ivory felt
- Craft glue

Instructions

1. Cut plastic canvas according to graphs. Cut two pieces felt slightly smaller than plastic canvas.

2. Using two strands pearl cotton, stitch front and back following graphs. Work Backstitches with 6 strands metallic floss.

3. Overcast top edges from blue dot to blue dot with two strands light beige gray pearl cotton. Attach beads with sewing thread and needle.

4. Place small line of glue around edge of one piece of felt and glue to wrong side of nosegay front. Repeat with remaining piece of felt and nosegay back.

5. With two strands light beige gray pearl cotton, Whipstitch nosegay front to nosegay back around side and bottom edges from dot to dot.

6. Thread cord through large-eye needle and tie a knot in one end. On right side of nosegay and approximately 1" from top, bring needle from inside to outside, pulling cord until knot is secured against the inside seam. Insert needle back into Whipstitched edge ¼" above knot; pull firmly.

7. On left side of nosegay approximately ¾" from top, bring needle from inside to outside. Insert needle back into Whipstitched edge ¼" below exit point. Pull cord out enough to knot end, then pull on cord until knot is secured against inside seam.

8. Using photo as a guide, arrange flowers, cutting stems to fit in nosegay. If desired, glue flowers in place. ❖

COLOR KEY	
#3 Pearl Cotton	**Yards**
▨ Blue green #502	1
☐ Light wedgewood #518	1
■ Dark carnation #601	1
▨ Light cranberry #603	1
☐ Light beige gray #822	16
Uncoded areas are light beige gray #822 Continental Stitches	
6-Strand Divisible Metallic Floss	
╱ Silver #5283 Backstitch	3
○ Attach yellow glass bead	
Color numbers given are for DMC #3 pearl cotton and 6-strand divisible metallic floss.	

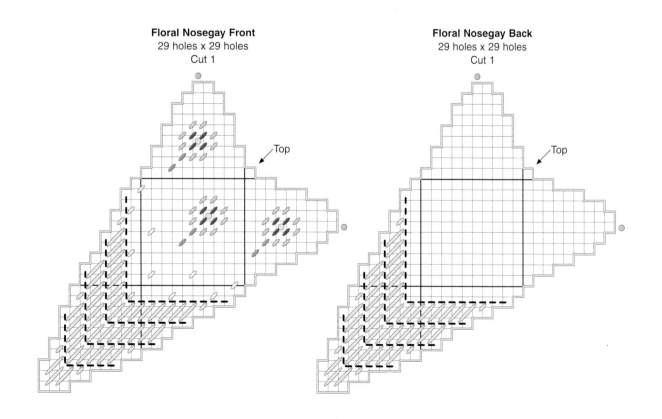

Floral Nosegay Front
29 holes x 29 holes
Cut 1

Floral Nosegay Back
29 holes x 29 holes
Cut 1

Skill Level: Beginner

Materials
Each Project
- 1 sheet Darice Ultimate 7-count plastic canvas
- 3" plastic canvas radial circle

Mom's Set
- Red Heart Super Saver worsted weight yarn Art. E301 as listed in color key

- Red Heart Classic worsted weight yarn Art. E267 as listed in color key

Dad's Set
- Spinrite Bernat Berella "4" worsted weight yarn as listed in color key

Instructions
1. Cut plastic canvas according to graphs (right and page 68). Coaster bottom and 3" radial circles will remain unstitched.

2. Stitch covers following graphs, overlapping three holes where indicated before stitching. With eggshell, Overcast top edge of mom's can cover; Whipstitch bottom edge to circle using two stitches per hole in circle as necessary. Repeat for dad's can cover, Overcasting and Whipstitching with beige.

Beverage Sets

Designs by Brandon J. Wiant

Stitch up these attractive beverage sets including can cover, straw cover and coaster for Mom and Dad to use at work or at play.

to dot. Whipstitch wrong sides of corresponding straw covers together along side edges between dots.

5. Following graphs, stitch two of dad's straw covers with light teal, two with honey, two with oak and two with warm brown.

Using beige throughout, Overcast top edges from dot to dot, bottom edges from dot to dot and center of sides from dot to dot. Whipstitch wrong sides of corresponding straw covers together along unstitched side edges. ❖

Mom's Straw Ornament
6 holes x 6 holes
Cut 8
Stitch 2 as graphed,
2 with peacock green,
2 with pale rose,
2 with light berry

Dad's Straw Ornament
6 holes x 6 holes
Cut 8
Stitch 2 as graphed,
2 with honey, 2 with oak,
2 with warm brown

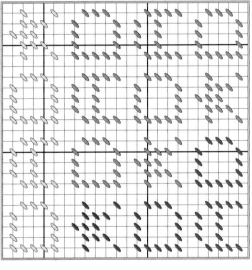

Dad's Coaster Top & Bottom
24 holes x 24 holes
Cut 2, stitch 1

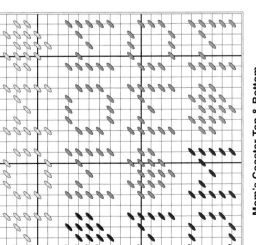

Mom's Coaster Top & Bottom
24 holes x 24 holes
Cut 2, stitch 1

3. Stitch coaster tops following graphs. Whipstitch mom's coaster top and bottom together with off-white and dad's together with beige.

4. Following graphs, stitch two of mom's straw covers with raspberry, two with peacock green, two with pale rose and two with light berry. Using off-white throughout, Overcast top edges from dot to dot and bottom edges from dot

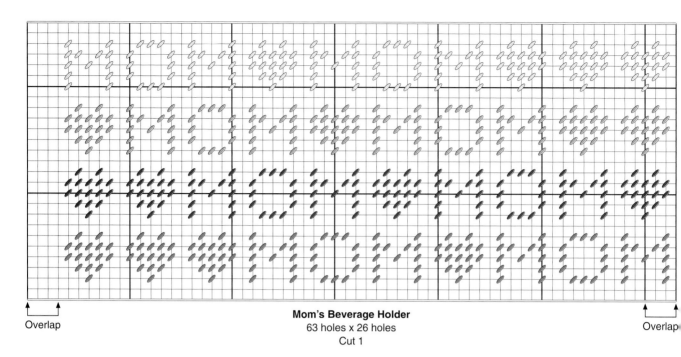

Mom's Beverage Holder
63 holes x 26 holes
Cut 1

Overlap

Overlap

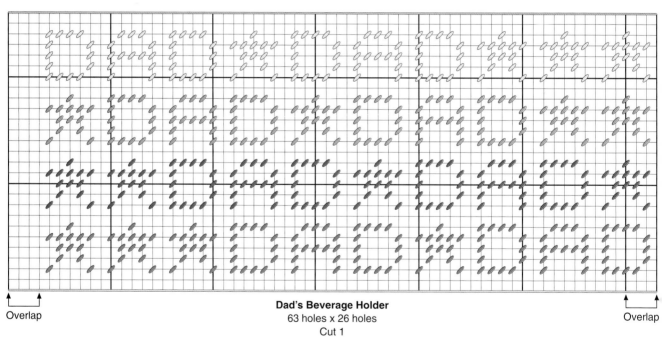

Dad's Beverage Holder
63 holes x 26 holes
Cut 1

Overlap

Overlap

COLOR KEY
DAD'S BEVERAGE SET

Worsted Weight Yarn	Yards
☐ Honey #8795	4
◩ Oak #8796	4
■ Warm brown #8797	4
◪ Light teal #8845	4
Uncoded areas are beige #8764 Continental Stitches	26
╱ Beige #8764 Overcasting and Whipstitching	

Color numbers given are for Spinrite Bernat Berella "4" worsted weight yarn.

COLOR KEY
MOM'S BEVERAGE SET

Worsted Weight Yarn	Yards
◩ Raspberry #375	4
■ Peacock green #508	4
☐ Pale rose #755	4
■ Light berry #761	4
Uncoded areas are off-white #3 Continental Stitches	26
╱ Off-white #3 Overcasting and Whipstitching	

Color numbers given are for Red Heart Classic worsted weight yarn Art. E267 and Super Saver yarn Art. E301.

ARROWHEAD DESK SET

Designs by Ruby Thacker

Dad will be pleasantly surprised when he opens this Father's Day gift! A striking arrowhead design worked in vibrant colors makes this box and photo frame a gift set he'll appreciate.

Skill Level: Intermediate

Materials

Each Project

- 2 sheets stiff plastic canvas
- Uniek Needloft plastic canvas yarn as listed in color key
- Leather lacing as listed in color key
- 8 gold pony beads
- Craft glue

Covered Box

- 1⅞" x 1⅜" gold oval concho

Picture Frame

- Monofilament (optional)

Project Note

When working with black leather lacing, keep lacing smooth and flat by guiding it between the thumb and forefinger of free hand.

Arrowhead Box

1. Cut plastic canvas according to graphs (pages 70–72). Carefully cut out slits on lid top. Cut one 42-hole x 42-hole piece for box bottom. Box bottom will remain unstitched.

2. Stitch lid top following graph. Thread leather lacing up and down through slits on lid top as indicated. At each corner, come up in one corner slit, thread on one bead, tie a knot in lacing, thread on another gold bead, and go down through next corner slit. Trim lacing ends; glue in place on wrong side.

3. Thread two 6" lengths of lacing through concho and knot at center of concho. Glue to center of lid top.

4. Stitch lid sides following graphs. **Note:** *Each side has a different design. Stitch as shown so sides will match top.* Using red, Whipstitch lid sides together in proper sequence. Whipstitch sides to lid; Overcast bottom edge of lid sides.

5. Stitch box sides following graphs. **Note:** *Each side has a different design to match lid sides.* With red, Whipstitch sides together in proper sequence;

Whipstitch sides to bottom; Overcast top edge of sides. Place lid on box, matching sides.

Arrowhead Frame

1. Cut plastic canvas according to graphs (page 72), choosing either a stand or hanger. Cut out slits and photo opening from frame front only. Frame back, stand and hanger will remain unstitched.

2. Stitch frame front following graph. Overcast edges of photo opening with gray. Do not Overcast edges of slits. Thread leather lacing around frame following instructions for step 2 of Arrowhead Box.

3. Using monofilament or yarn, center and Whipstitch bottom edge of hanger to seventh bar from the top on frame back, or center and Whipstitch long straight edge of stand to frame back, making sure bottom edges are even.

4. Using red throughout, Overcast bottom edge of frame front. With wrong sides together, Whipstitch frame front to frame back around side and top edges. ❖

COLOR KEY	
ARROWHEAD BOX	
Plastic Canvas Yarn	**Yards**
■ Black #00	21
■ Red #01	33
▨ Gray #38	23
☐ White #41	41
Leather Lacing	
╱ Black	1
Color numbers given are for Uniek Needloft plastic canvas yarn.	

Whipstitch to box lid top side 1

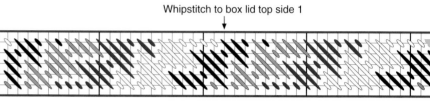

Arrowhead Box Lid Side 1
44 holes x 6 holes
Cut 1

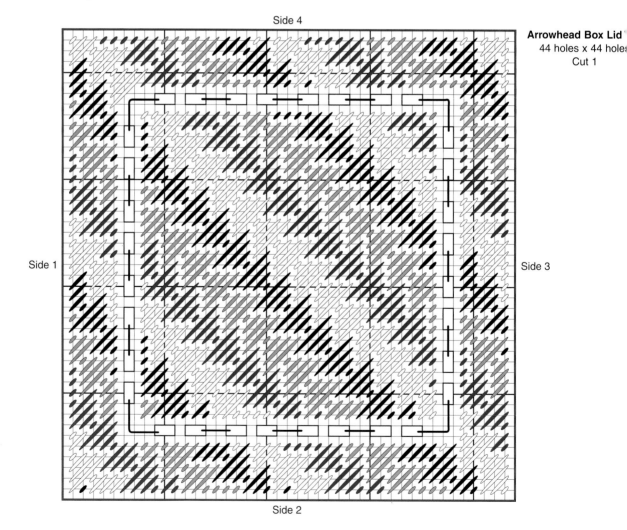

Side 4

Side 1

Side 3

Side 2

Arrowhead Box Lid
44 holes x 44 holes
Cut 1

Whipstitch to box lid top side 2

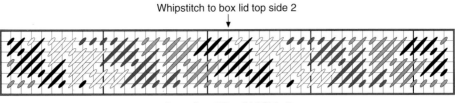

Arrowhead Box Lid Side 2
44 holes x 6 holes
Cut 1

Whipstitch to box lid top side 3

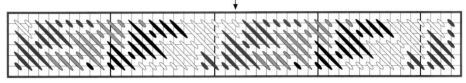

Arrowhead Box Lid Side 3
44 holes x 6 holes
Cut 1

Whipstitch to box lid top side 4

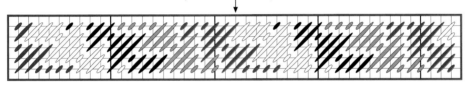

Arrowhead Box Lid Side 4
44 holes x 6 holes
Cut 1

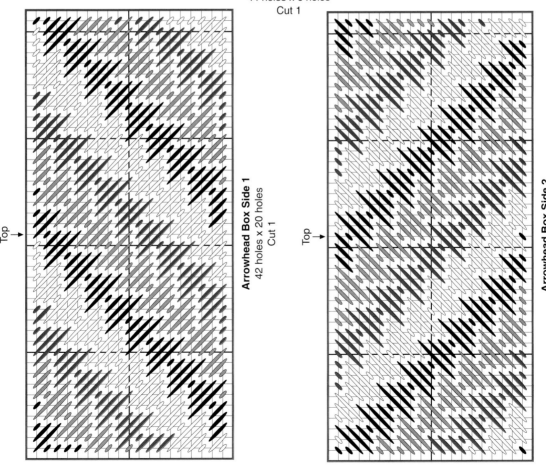

Top →

Arrowhead Box Side 1
42 holes x 20 holes
Cut 1

Top →

Arrowhead Box Side 2
42 holes x 20 holes
Cut 1

Cut out for front only

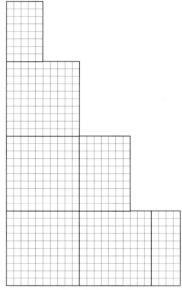

Arrowhead Frame Hanger
9 holes x 4 holes
Cut 1
Do not stitch

COLOR KEY
ARROWHEAD FRAME

Plastic Canvas Yarn	Yards
■ Black #00	6
■ Red #01	8
▨ Gray #38	18
□ White #41	6
Leather Lacing	
╱ Black	1

Color numbers given are for Uniek Needloft plastic canvas yarn.

Arrowhead Frame Front & Back
51 holes x 65 holes
Cut 2, stitch 1

Arrowhead Frame Stand
24 holes x 38 holes
Cut 1
Do not stitch

Top

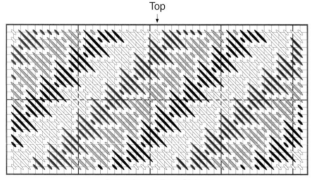

Arrowhead Box Side 3
42 holes x 20 holes
Cut 1

Top

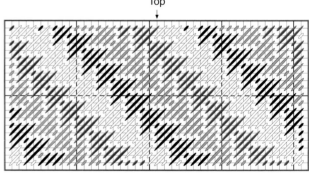

Arrowhead Box Side 4
42 holes x 20 holes
Cut 1

Delight your mom and dad on their special days with these colorful celebration banners. Mom's is accented with pretty hummingbirds while Dad's features handsome mallard ducks.

Skill Level: Intermediate

Materials

Each Banner

- 4 sheets 7-count plastic canvas
- Darice Nylon Plus plastic canvas yarn as listed in color key
- 2 (¾") white plastic rings
- Craft glue or glue gun

Hummingbirds

- 2 (5mm) black cabochons
- Black chenille stem

Ducks

- 2 (6mm) black cabochons

Hummingbirds

1. Cut two banner pieces, two of each streamer, two hummingbirds and two wings from plastic canvas according to graphs (pages 75–77). One banner and one of each streamer will remain unstitched for backing.

2. Cross Stitch words on banner and streamer fronts with purple following graphs; stitch uncoded backgrounds with white Continental Stitches.

3. Attach one plastic ring to top backside of each streamer back with white yarn where indicated on graphs. Using purple, Whip-stitch banner front to banner back and streamer backs to streamer fronts.

4. Stitch one hummingbird and one wing following graphs; reverse plastic canvas and direction of stitches for remaining bird and wing. Overcast wings with forest green and birds with adjacent colors following graph.

5. Using photo as a guide through step 7, glue tops of streamers behind ends of banner.

6. Cut four 2" lengths of chenille stem. Glue one stem behind each bird for its bill. Bend remaining two stems to

resemble feet; glue in place to backs of birds.

7. Glue one cabochon to each bird where indicated on graph. Glue wings to birds. Glue birds to top ends of banners.

Ducks

1. Cut two banner pieces, two of each streamer, one female duck, one female duck wing, one male duck and one male duck wing from plastic canvas according to graphs (pages 75–77). One banner and one of each streamer will remain unstitched for backing.

2. Cross Stitch words on banner

and streamer fronts with royal dark blue following graphs; stitch uncoded backgrounds with sandstone Continental Stitches.

3. Attach one plastic ring to top backside of each streamer back with sandstone yarn where indicated on graphs. Using royal dark blue, Whipstitch banner front to banner back and streamer backs to streamer fronts.

4. Stitch ducks and wings following graphs. Work Backstitches when background stitching is completed. Overcast following graphs.

5. Using photo as a guide through step 6, glue tops of streamers behind ends of banner.

6. Glue one cabochon to each duck where indicated on graph. Glue wings to ducks. Glue ducks to top ends of banners. ❖

Male Duck Wing
18 holes x 10 holes
Cut 1

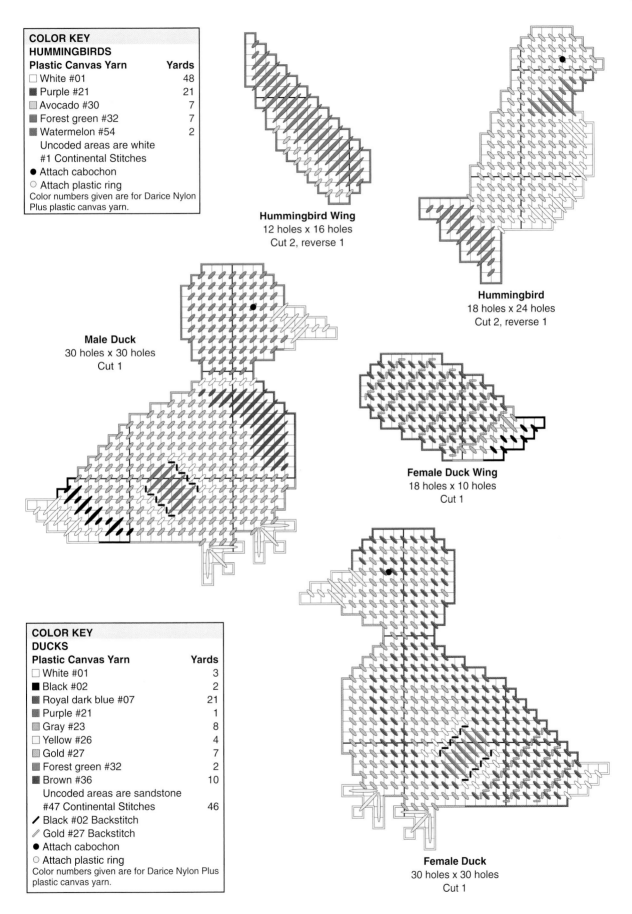

COLOR KEY
HUMMINGBIRDS

Plastic Canvas Yarn	Yards
☐ White #01	48
■ Purple #21	21
☐ Avocado #30	7
■ Forest green #32	7
■ Watermelon #54	2

Uncoded areas are white
#1 Continental Stitches
● Attach cabochon
○ Attach plastic ring
Color numbers given are for Darice Nylon
Plus plastic canvas yarn.

Hummingbird Wing
12 holes x 16 holes
Cut 2, reverse 1

Hummingbird
18 holes x 24 holes
Cut 2, reverse 1

Male Duck
30 holes x 30 holes
Cut 1

Female Duck Wing
18 holes x 10 holes
Cut 1

COLOR KEY
DUCKS

Plastic Canvas Yarn	Yards
☐ White #01	3
■ Black #02	2
■ Royal dark blue #07	21
■ Purple #21	1
☐ Gray #23	8
☐ Yellow #26	4
☐ Gold #27	7
■ Forest green #32	2
■ Brown #36	10
Uncoded areas are sandstone #47 Continental Stitches	46
╱ Black #02 Backstitch	
╱ Gold #27 Backstitch	
● Attach cabochon	
○ Attach plastic ring	

Color numbers given are for Darice Nylon Plus
plastic canvas yarn.

Female Duck
30 holes x 30 holes
Cut 1

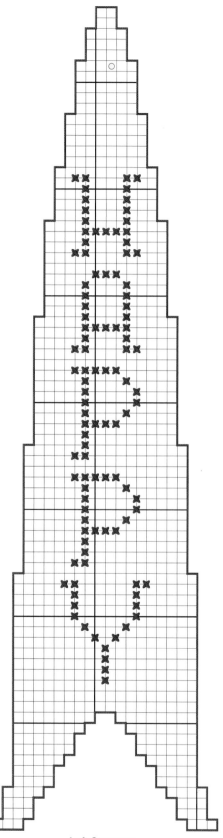

Left Streamer
22 holes x 77 holes
Cut 2, stitch 1, for Mother's Banner
Stitch as graphed
Cut 2, stitch 1, for Father's Banner,
replacing purple with royal dark blue

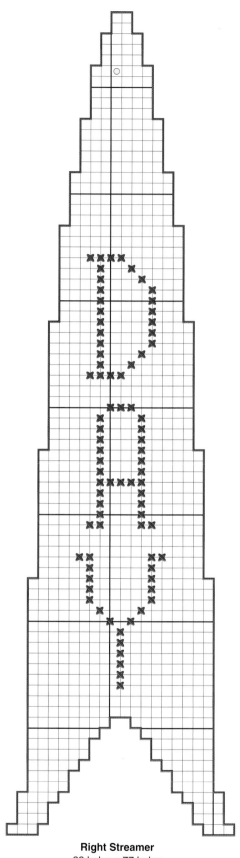

Right Streamer
22 holes x 77 holes
Cut 2, stitch 1, for Mother's Banner
Stitch as graphed
Cut 2, stitch 1, for Father's Banner,
replacing purple with royal dark blue

Mother's Banner
89 holes x 38 holes
Cut 2, stitch 1

Father's Banner
89 holes x 38 holes
Cut 2, stitch 1

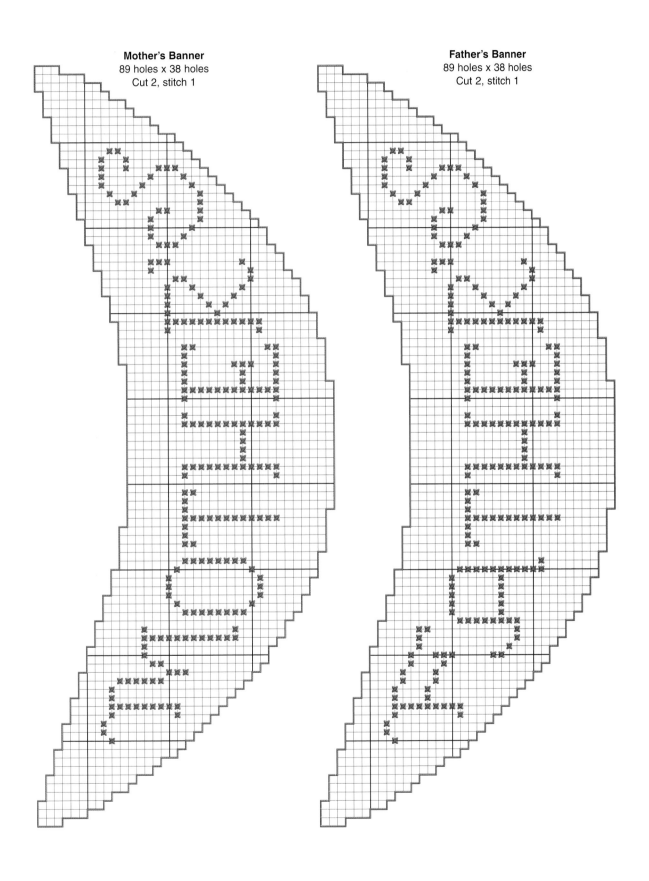

All-American Celebration

Whether your Fourth of July celebration is an indoor or outdoor affair, you'll have the perfect decorations and accessories for the event! Rockets, stars and stripes in red, white and blue will add eye-catching fun as you celebrate America's birthday!

Patriotic Welcome

Design by Vicki Blizzard • Shown on page 79

Hang this cheery surname sign on your front door to welcome guests while expressing your patriotism.

Skill Level: Beginner

Materials

- 2 sheets 7-count plastic canvas
- Uniek plastic canvas star shape
- Red Heart Super Saver worsted weight yarn Art. E301 as listed in color key
- Red Heart Classic worsted weight yarn Art. E267 as listed in color key
- #16 tapestry needle
- 1 yard ⅛"-wide navy blue satin ribbon
- Sawtooth hanger
- Hot-glue gun

Instructions

1. Cut plastic canvas according to graphs (right and page 89), cutting letters needed for desired name and cutting away shaded gray area on heart large star.

2. Following graphs, stitch name sign, large star, heart top and heart tip, overlapping holes on heart pieces where indicated before stitching. Overcast heart with cherry red and soft navy and name sign with soft navy following graphs.

3. Stitch and Overcast welcome and name-sign letters with soft navy and small stars with eggshell following graphs.

4. Cut a 12" length of navy blue ribbon. Thread ends from back to front through holes indicated at bottom of heart; pull ribbon so ends are even. Thread one end from front to back through hole indicated on left side of

name sign; knot end on backside. Repeat for remaining end, threading through hole indicated on right side of name sign.

5. Cut three 6" lengths of navy blue ribbon. Tie each length in a small bow; trim ends as desired. Glue one bow to each top corner of name sign. Glue remaining

bow to bottom of heart.

6. Using photo as a guide, glue welcome letters to heart; center and glue letters to name sign. Glue large star to center of blue area on heart, then glue small stars around large star.

7. Center and glue sawtooth hanger to backside of heart. ❖

COLOR KEY	
Worsted Weight Yarn	**Yards**
■ Soft navy #853	23
☐ Eggshell #111	36
■ Cherry red #912	27
● Attach ribbon	
Color numbers given are for Red Heart Super Saver worsted weight yarn Art. E301 and Red Heart Classic worsted weight yarn Art. E267.	

Patriotic Welcome Small Star
3 holes x 3 holes
Cut 10

Name Sign Letters

ABCDEFGHI
JKLMNOPQR
STUVWXYZ

Patriotic Welcome Heart Letters
7 holes x 9 holes

WELCOM

Cut 1   Cut 2   Cut 1   Cut 1   Cut 1   Cut 1

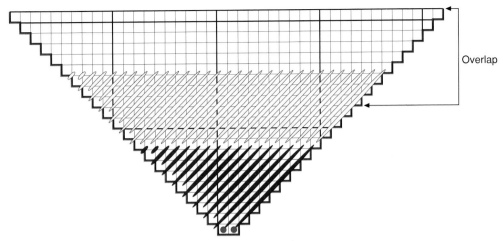

Patriotic Welcome Heart Tip
42 holes x 21 holes
Cut 1

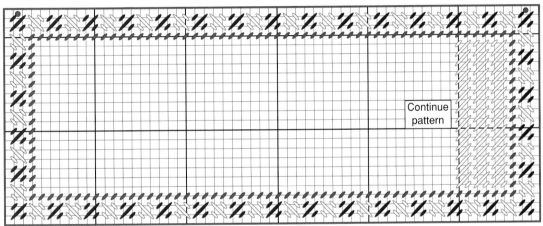

Continue
pattern

Patriotic Welcome Name Sign
59 holes x 23 holes
Cut 1

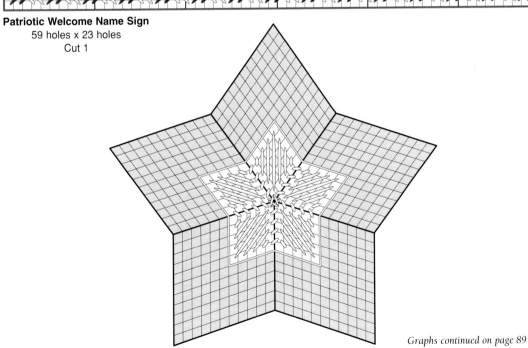

Patriotic Welcome Large Star
Cut 1

Graphs continued on page 89

Stars & S

Designs by Vicki Blizzard

This colorful set includes a nifty utensil and napkin caddy plus two weights for holding your paper plates and tablecloth on a breezy summer's day!

Picnic Set

Skill Level: Intermediate

Materials

- 2 sheets Uniek Quick-Count 7-count stiff plastic canvas
- 1 sheet Uniek Quick-Count 7-count clear plastic canvas
- ½ sheet Uniek Quick-Count 7-count white plastic canvas
- 3 Uniek plastic canvas star shapes
- Uniek Needloft plastic canvas yarn as listed in color key
- Uniek Needloft metallic craft cord as listed in color key
- #16 tapestry needle
- 2 sheets white felt
- 13 (3mm) round gold beads from The Beadery
- Sewing needle and clear thread
- 8-ounce package plastic pellets
- Hot-glue gun

Caddy

1. Cut away shaded gray area from two star shapes; cut two caddy long

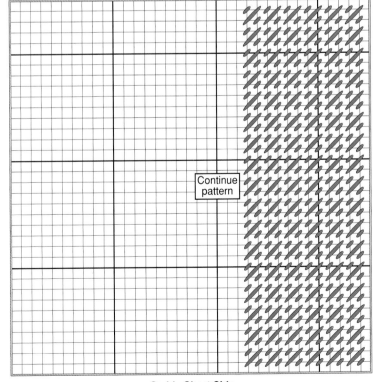

Caddy Short Side
35 holes x 35 holes
Cut 2 from stiff

sides and two caddy short sides from stiff plastic canvas; cut one handle from clear plastic canvas according to graphs.

2. Cut one 54-hole x 35-hole piece from stiff plastic canvas for caddy bottom. Cut one 52-hole x 33-hole piece and two 17-hole x 33-hole pieces from white plastic canvas for caddy dividers. Bottom and dividers will remain unstitched.

3. Stitch pieces following graphs. Overcast handle and stars with solid gold. Using sewing needle and clear thread, attach beads to star centers where indicated on graph.

4. Cut felt slightly smaller than sides and handle; glue felt to wrong side of each piece. Using solid gold throughout, Whipstitch sides together, then Whipstitch sides to bottom. Overcast top edges.

5. With dark royal, Whipstitch one small divider to 17th bar from left end on large center divider. Whipstitch second small divider to 17th bar from right end on large center divider. *Note: There should be 17 bars between small dividers.*

6. Place divider in caddy, center and tack in place on caddy bottom; glue tops of dividers in place to lining on sides. Glue handle ends to right sides of caddy short sides. Center and glue one star to each short side, overlapping handle slightly.

Weights

1. Cut away shaded gray area from one star shape; cut weight pieces from clear plastic canvas according to graphs. Weight bottoms will remain unstitched.

2. Stitch pieces following graphs. Overcast star with solid gold. Using sewing needle and clear thread, attach bead to star center where indicated on graph.

3. With wrong sides together, Whipstitch one weight front to one weight back with solid gold, filling with one half package of pellets before closing. Repeat with remaining weight. Center and glue star to top of dark royal weight. ❖

COLOR KEY

Plastic Canvas Yarn	Yards
■ Christmas red #02	32
□ White #41	35
■ Dark royal #48	58
Metallic Craft Cord	
▨ Solid gold #20	13
● Attach gold bead	

Color numbers given are for Uniek Needloft plastic canvas yarn and metallic craft cord.

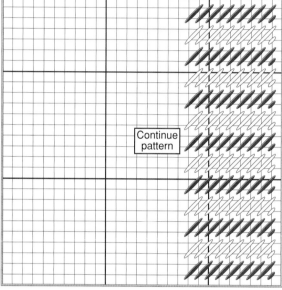

Striped Weight
27 holes x 27 holes
Cut 2, stitch 1, from clear regular

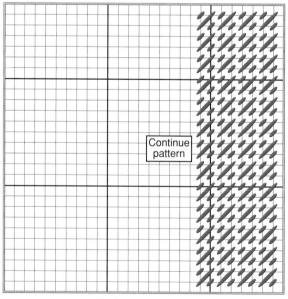

Dark Royal Weight
27 holes x 27 holes
Cut 2, stitch 1, from clear regular

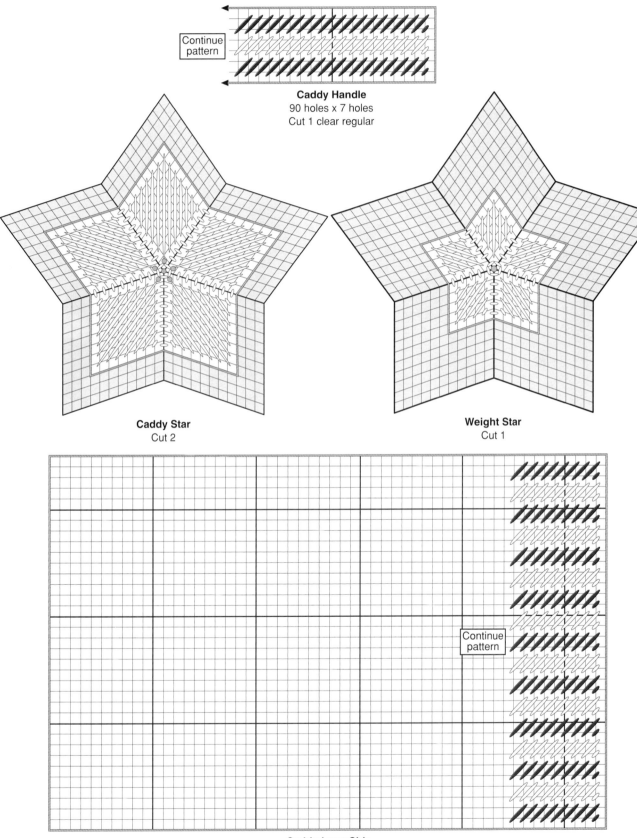

Caddy Handle
90 holes x 7 holes
Cut 1 clear regular

Continue
pattern

Caddy Star
Cut 2

Weight Star
Cut 1

Continue
pattern

Caddy Long Side
54 holes x 35 holes
Cut 2 from stiff

You won't want to start your family's July 4th picnic without this dazzling centerpiece, featuring five colorful rockets blasting into the air!

Skill Level: Beginner

Materials

- ½ sheet 7-count plastic canvas
- 2 (6") 7-count plastic canvas radial circles
- Darice Straw Satin Raffia Cord as listed in color key
- 36" ⅛"-diameter wooden dowel
- White acrylic paint
- Large metallic spray picks: 2 gold and 1 silver
- Small metallic spray picks: 2 gold and 2 silver
- Floral clay
- White paper
- Low-temperature glue gun

Cutting & Stitching

1. For base sides, cut both radial circles in half along center bar. Discard halves without center bar. Cut remaining pieces from plastic canvas according to graphs (page 88).

2. Stitch base end caps, base bottom, rockets and small nose cones following graphs. Stitch four large nose cones with red as graphed; stitch two replacing red with dark blue. Work Backstitches on cones when background stitching is completed.

3. With white, Long Stitch one half-circle from the center (first) row of holes to the fourth row of holes with white. Continuing outward, Long Stitch with red around half-circle from the fourth row of holes to the seventh row of holes, using two stitches per hole as necessary to cover canvas.

4. Repeat four more times from the seventh row to the 10th with white, from the 10th to the 13th with red, from the 13th to the 16th with white and from the 16th to the outside row of holes with red. Repeat with second half-circle.

5. Using adjacent colors throughout, Overcast bottom edges of nose cones. Whipstitch wrong sides of each pair of nose cones together along side edges.

6. Using white through step 7, Overcast bottom edges of each rocket piece. Whipstitch wrong sides of each pair of rockets together along side and top edges.

7. Overcast base end caps, short edges of base bottom and round edge of half-circles. With wrong sides facing inside, Whipstitch long edges of bottom to straight edges of half-circles.

Assembly

1. Cut dowel into three 8" lengths and two 6" lengths. Paint all dowel pieces white. Allow to dry.

2. Form a piece of floral clay to fit on base bottom; wrap with white paper. Glue to inside of base bottom.

3. Glue nose cones over tops of corresponding rockets. Glue metallic sprays and dowels into bottoms of rockets as follows: one large dowel and one large gold spray into each large side rocket; one large dowel and one large silver spray into center rocket; and one small dowel, one small silver spray and one small gold spray into each small rocket.

4. Using photo as a guide throughout, cut small holes for dowels in top of white paper. Insert bottoms of dowels into floral clay at holes. Glue top edges of base sides to dowels. Glue base end caps to bottom and sides of base. ❖

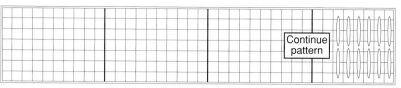

Base Bottom
7 holes x 38 holes
Cut 1

COLOR KEY

Straw Satin Raffia Cord	Yards
☐ White #3401-01	24
■ Red #3401-04	18
■ Dark blue #3401-16	10
⟋ White #3401-01 Backstitch	
⟋ Red #3401-04 Backstitch	

Color numbers given are for Darice Straw Satin Raffia Cord.

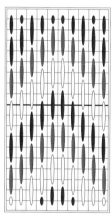

Large Center Rocket
10 holes x 19 holes
Cut 2

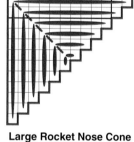

Large Rocket Nose Cone
12 holes x 12 holes
Cut 6
Stitch 4 as graphed
for large side rockets
Stitch 2 with dark blue
for large center rocket

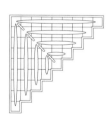

Small Rocket Nose Cone
9 holes x 9 holes
Cut 4

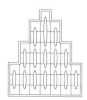

Base End Cap
7 holes x 8 holes
Cut 2

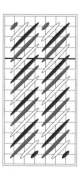

Small Rocket
7 holes x 14 holes
Cut 4

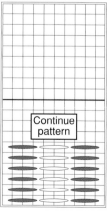

Large Side Rocket
10 holes x 19 holes
Cut 4

Patriotic Welcome

Continued from page 81

COLOR KEY

Worsted Weight Yarn	Yards
■ Soft navy #853	23
□ Eggshell #111	36
■ Cherry red #912	27
● Attach ribbon	

Color numbers given are for Red Heart
Super Saver worsted weight yarn Art.
E301 and Red Heart Classic worsted
weight yarn Art. E267.

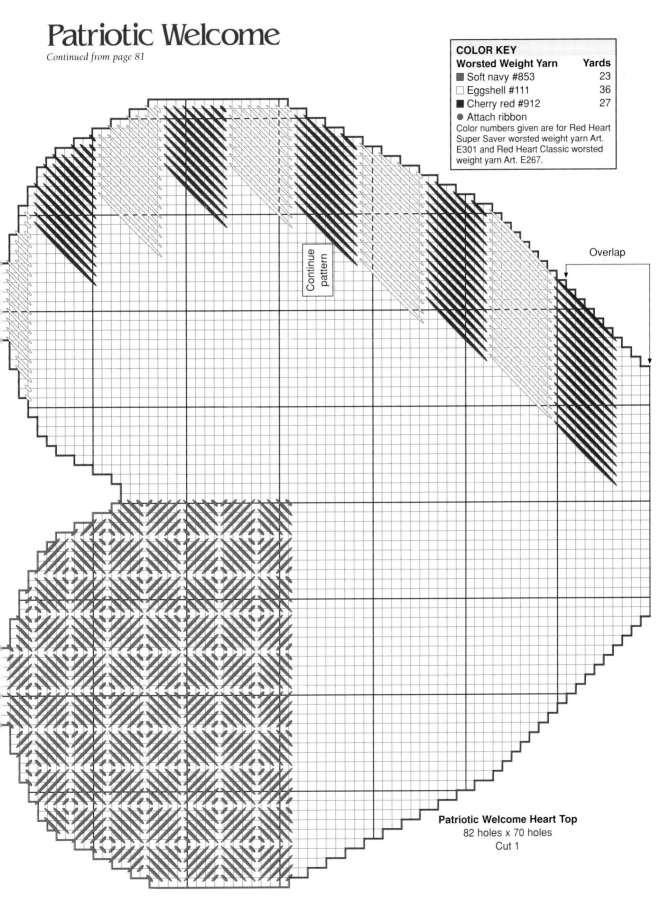

Continue pattern

Overlap

Patriotic Welcome Heart Top
82 holes x 70 holes
Cut 1

POCKET COASTERS

Designs by Kathy Wirth

With a handy pocket holder accented with country embellishments, this coaster set can be stitched in just a couple of hours!

Skill Level: Beginner

Materials

- 1½ sheets ivory 7-count plastic canvas
- Uniek Needloft plastic canvas yarn as listed in color key
- GlissenGloss 4mm Braid Ribbon 4 by Madeira as listed in color key
- #16 tapestry needle
- 9" x 12" sheet adhesive-backed red felt
- ¾" metallic gold shank button
- Small amount natural raffia
- Emery board
- Craft glue

Instructions

1. Cut plastic canvas according to graphs. Cut four 3⅞" squares from red felt.

2. Stitch pieces with yarn following graphs, using long lengths of yarn to work each of the four top stripes on pocket as they will show from both sides. Do not carry yarn across

unstitched areas of pocket.

3. Stitch with braid ribbon, keeping ribbon flat by guiding between thumb and forefinger. Do not Overcast edges of coasters and pocket.

4. Using straw yarn throughout and with wrong side facing up, tie points A, B and C of pocket together at center, knotting securely and leaving a 7" tail in front. Attach button just below center on front. Tack lower corners closed, knotting yarn on the inside.

COLOR KEY

Plastic Canvas Yarn	Yards
☐ Straw #19	13
■ Crimson #42	28
▨ Dark royal #48	15
4mm Braid Ribbon	
☐ Dark gold #01	10

Color numbers given are for Uniek Needloft plastic canvas yarn and GlissenGloss Braid Ribbon 4 by Madeira.

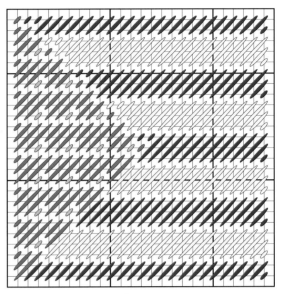

Coaster
26 holes x 26 holes
Cut 4

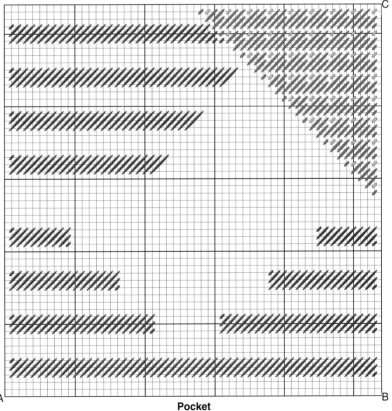

Pocket
54 holes x 54 holes
Cut 1

5. Anchor a 7" length of straw yarn at point on upper flap; dab glue on backside to secure. Place a small amount of glue on yarn knot behind button to secure. Roll tail ends of both 7" lengths of yarn in glue to prevent fraying.

6. Place three pieces of raffia together; tie in a bow around button shank. Trim ends as desired.

7. Remove backing from felt and place on backsides of stitched coasters. Smooth plastic canvas on corners of coasters with emery board. ❖

HANDY
Can Covers

Designs by Ruby Thacker

Make a dozen or more of these attractive and practical soda can covers. They give a better grip and are pleasing to the eyes, too.

Skill Level: Beginner

Materials

- 1 sheet 7-count plastic canvas
- 2 (3") plastic canvas radial circles
- Uniek Needloft plastic canvas yarn as listed in color key

Instructions

1. Cut plastic canvas according to graphs.

2. Stitch pieces following graphs, overlapping five holes before stitching.

3. Using dark royal, Overcast top edge of Stripes holder; Whipstitch bottom edge to one 3" circle. Using white, Overcast top edge of Stars holder; Whipstitch bottom edge to remaining 3" circle. ❖

COLOR KEY	
Plastic Canvas Yarn	**Yards**
■ Red #01	20
☐ White #41	25
▨ Dark royal #48	20
Uncoded areas are white #41 Continental Stitches	
Color numbers given are for Uniek Needloft plastic canvas yarn.	

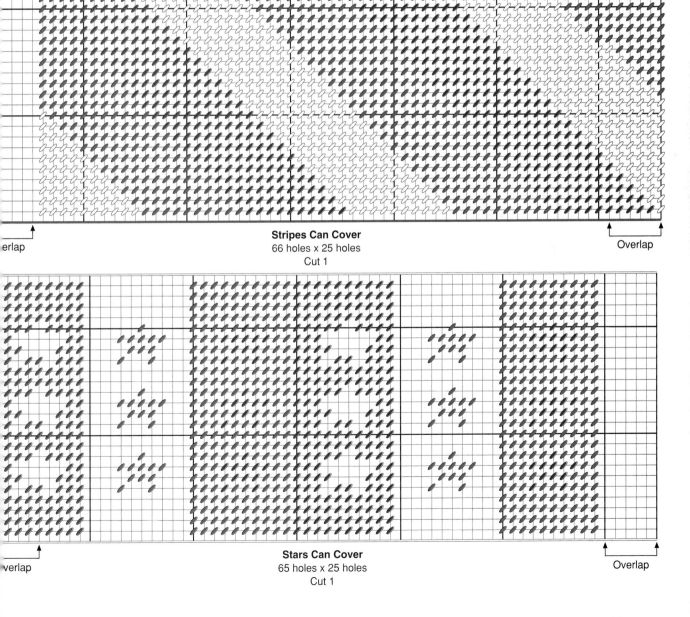

Stripes Can Cover
66 holes x 25 holes
Cut 1

Overlap

Overlap

Stars Can Cover
65 holes x 25 holes
Cut 1

Overlap

Overlap

Happy Halloween

Stitch a treat for your little ghosts and goblins this Halloween! Whimsical decorations and party favors will keep them coming back for more spooky fun!

Witch's Brew centerpiece

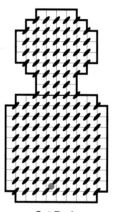

Skill Level: Advanced

Materials

- 1½ sheets 7-count plastic canvas
- ¼ sheet 10-count plastic canvas
- 2 (6") plastic canvas radial circles
- 3" plastic canvas radial circle
- #16 tapestry needle
- #22 tapestry needle
- Red Heart Classic worsted weight yarn Art. E267 as listed in color key
- Red Heart Sport sport weight yarn Art. E289 as listed in color key
- Anchor 6-strand embroidery floss as listed in color key
- Kreinik Heavy (#32) Braid: 2 yards black #005
- 6 (¼") black pompoms
- 4 (7mm) black pompoms
- 3 (5mm) round black cabochons
- 2 (7mm) movable eyes
- 2 (6mm) yellow animal eyes with shanks
- Black chenille wire
- Wire cutters
- Pencil
- Fabric stiffener spray
- Tape
- 1 yard ⅛"-wide purple satin ribbon
- 1 yard ¹⁄₁₆"-wide purple satin ribbon
- 8 brass charms: stars, keys, locks, clock

Design by Vicki Blizzard • Shown on page 95

This scary witch is brewing up a secret potion to send shivers up the spines of one and all! Use her with a battery-operated candle to add a spooky glow to your Halloween table!

- 4 black pony beads
- Fiberfill
- 2 cups stuffing pellets
- Plastic sandwich bag
- Sheet black felt
- 7" battery-operated ornamental candle
- Ceramic buttons from Mill Hill Products by Gay Bowles Sales, Inc.:
  2 ghosts #86024
  4 pumpkin hearts #86083
  4 large pumpkin hearts #86163
- Sewing needle and off-white thread
- Hot-glue gun

Project Note

Stitch 7-count with #16 tapestry needle and 10-count with #22 tapestry needle.

Cat

1. Cut two bodies, two legs and two ears from 7-count plastic canvas according to graphs.

2. Stitch pieces following graphs. Using black yarn throughout, Overcast legs and ears, Whip-

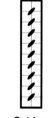

Cat Body
10 holes x 18 holes
Cut 2 from 7-count

Cat Leg
2 holes x 10 holes
Cut 2 from 7-count

Join

Cat Ear
3 holes x 2 holes
Cut 2 from 7-count

stitching bottom dart of each ear together as indicated while Overcasting. Whipstitch wrong sides of body pieces together, stuffing firmly with fiberfill before closing.

3. Cut chenille wire in half with wire cutters. Glue one end in body back in green hole indicated on graph. Curl wire as desired for tail.

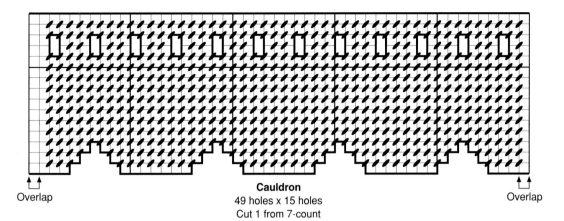

Cauldron
49 holes x 15 holes
Cut 1 from 7-count

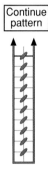

Continue
pattern

Cauldron Broomstick
2 holes x 45 holes
Cut 2 from 7-count

4. Using photo as a guide through step 6, glue ears to top corners of head. Center and glue two ¼" black pompoms side by side to bottom part of face for muzzle; glue one 5mm cabochon to center top of muzzle for nose.

5. Cut shanks off animal eyes and glue to face above muzzle. Making sure bottom edges are even, glue one 7mm black pompom to each leg for front feet; glue remaining two 7mm black pompoms to bottom front at side for back feet. Glue legs to body front.

6. Cut a 12" length of ⅛"-wide ribbon; tie around cat's neck. Thread one charm on each end of ribbon; slide charms to neck and tie in another knot. Tie ribbon in a small bow; trim ends. Dot knot with glue to secure.

Cauldron

1. Cut one cauldron and two

broomsticks from 7-count plastic canvas according to graphs.

2. Stitch cauldron following graph. Using black through step 3, with right sides together, Whipstitch each of the 12 holes closed at top of cauldron. With wrong sides together, Whipstitch each dart at bottom together.

3. Roll cauldron into cylinder, overlapping side edges where indicated on graph; stitch overlap with Continental Stitches. Overcast top and bottom edges. Glue one pony bead to bottom of cauldron at each dart.

4. Stitch broomstick pieces following graph. Whipstitch wrong sides of stick pieces together with mid brown. Using photo as a guide through step 5, glue broomstick inside cauldron.

5. Place a line of hot glue inside cauldron around sides, approximately ½" from top edge. Place a small handful of fiberfill inside cauldron, pressing into hot glue. Pull puffs over top edge and down outside of cauldron to resemble steam.

Witch Face & Hands

1. Cut one face, two hands and two nose pieces from 10-count plastic canvas according to graphs.

2. Stitch pieces following graphs, reversing one hand and one nose before stitching. Work French

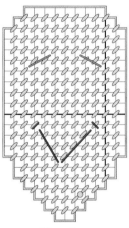

Witch Face
12 holes x 20 holes
Cut 1 from 10-count

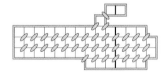

Witch Hand
14 holes x 6 holes
Cut 2, reverse 1, from 10-count

Witch Nose
3 holes x 5 holes
Cut 2, reverse 1, from 10-count

Knot wart on one nose piece only.

3. Using pale green throughout, Overcast face and hands. Whipstitch wrong sides of nose pieces together. Work embroidery on face, using 2 plies nickel yarn for eyebrows, 6 strands floss for mouth and pale green

COLOR KEY

Worsted Weight Yarn	Yards
■ Black #12	40
■ Mid brown #339	2
■ Nickel #401	26
■ Purple #596	29
╱ Nickel #401 2-ply Straight Stitch	
Sport Weight Yarn	
□ Pale green #685	5
○ Pale green #685 French Knot	
6-Strand Embroidery Floss	
╱ Dark red #9046 Backstitch	⅛
● Attach black chenille wire	
○ Attach sleeve fringe	
● Attach movable eye	

Color numbers given are for Red Heart Classic worsted weight yarn Art. E267, Red Heart sport weight yarn Art. E289 and Anchor 6-strand embroidery floss.

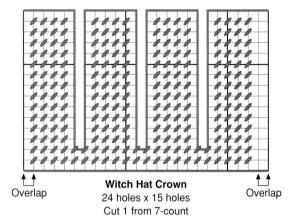

Witch Hat Crown
24 holes x 15 holes
Cut 1 from 7-count

Overlap   Overlap

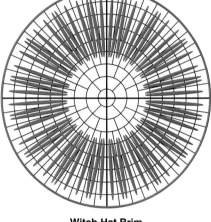

Witch Hat Brim
Stitch 1

yarn for French Knot wart.

4. Using photo as a guide, glue two 5mm black cabochons to face for eyes. Glue nose to face.

Witch Sleeves

1. Cut four sleeves from 7-count plastic canvas according to graph.

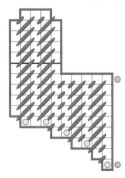

Witch Sleeve
10 holes x 15 holes
Cut 4, reverse 2, from 7-count

2. Stitch pieces following graph, reversing two sleeves before stitching. Using purple through-out, Overcast pieces from dot to dot along wrist edge. Matching edges, Whipstitch wrong sides of two sleeves together around remaining unstitched edges. Repeat with remaining two sleeves.

3. Glue hands inside sleeves. To curve hands, curl hands tightly, then release them.

4. Cut 10 (3") lengths of purple yarn; tie a knot in one end of each length. Thread one length

through each hole indicated on graph so tails are on outside of sleeve; pull until knot is next to plastic canvas. Unravel ends and trim as desired for fringe.

Witch Hat

1. Cut one hat crown from 7-count plastic canvas according to graph.

2. Stitch 3" circle for hat brim following graph. Overcast outside edge with purple, working two stitches in each hole to cover completely.

3. Stitch hat crown following graph. Using purple throughout and with wrong sides together, Whipstitch darts. Roll piece into a cylinder, overlapping side edges where indicated on graph; stitch overlap with Continental Stitches. Overcast top and bottom edge.

4. Glue hat crown over unstitched area of hat brim. Using photo as a guide, cut a length of ⅛"-wide purple ribbon to fit around base of hat crown; glue in place with ends overlapping at seam of hat. Cut a 6" length of ⅛"-wide purple ribbon and tie in a small bow; trim ends. With seam in back, glue bow to right side of hat front dart. Glue a star charm to hat brim directly under bow.

Witch Body

1. Cut one body piece from 7-

count plastic canvas according to graph.

2. Stitch body with purple following graph. Roll body into a tube, overlapping side edges where indicated on graph; stitch overlap with Continental Stitches. Overcast bottom edge with purple.

Fig. 1
Lark's Head Knot

3. Cut 23 (12") lengths of nickel yarn. Attach one length in each hole around top edge with a Lark's Head Knot (Fig. 1). Unravel each piece of yarn and trim to form hair and bangs.
Note: *Bangs are approximately 7*

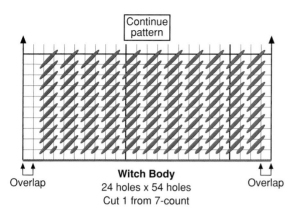

Continue pattern

Witch Body
24 holes x 54 holes
Cut 1 from 7-count

Overlap   Overlap

Spider Base
3 holes x 4 holes
Cut 4 from 7-count

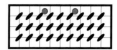

Goblin
10 holes x 4 holes
Cut 1 from 7-count

holes. Glue face to body with top edge under bangs; do not glue down chin. Shape face by curling chin up.

4. Cut a 6" length of ⅛"-wide purple ribbon and tie in a small bow; trim ends. Glue bow to body under chin.

5. Cut three 11"–12" lengths of ¹⁄₁₆"-wide purple ribbon; hold three pieces together and tie a knot in center. Tie ribbons around waist of body with knot in back. Tie remaining charms to ribbon ends, varying lengths; dot knots with glue to secure.

6. Using photo as a guide, glue one arm to each side of body, positioning arms so that one hand is slightly higher than the other. Glue hat to head, with front dart facing center.

Spiders

1. Cut four spider bases from 7-count plastic canvas following graph.

2. Stitch spider bases following graph; Overcast with black.

3. Tape one end of heavy (#32) braid to top of pencil. Spiral-wrap braid around pencil and tape other end to bottom of pencil. Spray braid heavily with fabric stiffener. Allow to dry for several hours.

4. Glue one ¼" black pompom to top of each spider base. When braid is completely dry, remove

tape and unwind from pencil. Roll braid tightly into coil, and cut through one side of coil to form curls. Glue curls to spider body to resemble legs; trim as necessary.

Base & Goblin

1. Cut one goblin and two base sides (page 102) from 7-count plastic canvas following graph. Using 6" circle as a template, cut a circle from black felt.

2. Stitch one 6" circle for base

top following graph. The 6" circle for base bottom will remain unstitched. Overcast 20 holes of base top with nickel.

3. Stitch base side following graph, overlapping four holes of two side pieces before stitching. Overlap and continue stitching remaining four holes on each short end, forming a circle.

4. With nickel, Whipstitch unstitched edges of base top to top edges of base side, Overcasting unstitched holes along top edge of base side that correspond with Overcast edges of base top.

5. Stitch and Overcast goblin with black following graph. Glue movable eyes to goblin where

Continued on page 102

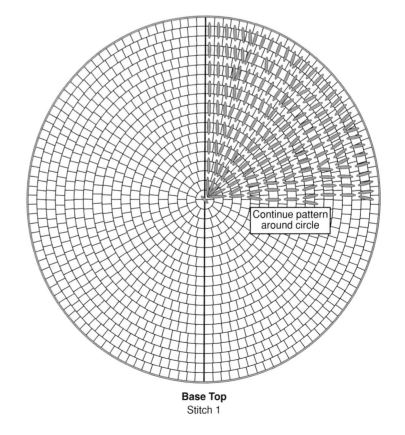

Base Top
Stitch 1

Continue pattern around circle

Pumpkin Patch

This charming door or wall welcome sign will add autumn cheer to your home throughout the fall season!

Skill Level: Beginner

Materials

- 1 sheet Darice Ultra Stiff 7-count plastic canvas
- Red Heart Classic worsted weight yarn Art. E267 as listed in color key
- DMC #3 pearl cotton as listed in color key
- Darice straw satin raffia cord: 4 yards natural #3401-07
- Small amount green Fun Foam craft foam by Westrim Crafts
- 8 pairs 5mm–12mm round and oval movable eyes
- 18" 20-gauge green floral stem wire
- Pencil or dowel
- Low-temperature glue gun

Instructions

1. Cut plastic canvas according to graphs (pages 101 and 103). Cut five large and three small pumpkin stems from green craft foam using patterns given.

2. Stitch pieces following graphs, reversing one large pumpkin and one medium pumpkin before stitching. Work uncoded areas on sign with eggshell Continental Stitches.

3. Work pearl cotton Backstitches over completed background stitching. Overcast pumpkins and fence with adjacent colors and sign with paddy green.

4. For straw at bottom of fence, bring natural raffia cord from front to back through first hole at bottom, leaving a 2" tail in the front. Come up through the third hole, pulling tight against the back. Go down in the second hole, leaving a 2" loop. Come up in the fifth hole, pulling tight, then down in the fourth, leaving a 2" loop. Continue pattern across bottom of fence.

5. Using photo as a guide through

Large Pumpkin Stem
Cut 5 from
green craft foam

Small Pumpkin Stem
Cut 3 from
green craft foam

Pumpkin Patch Fence
65 holes x 32 holes
Cut 1

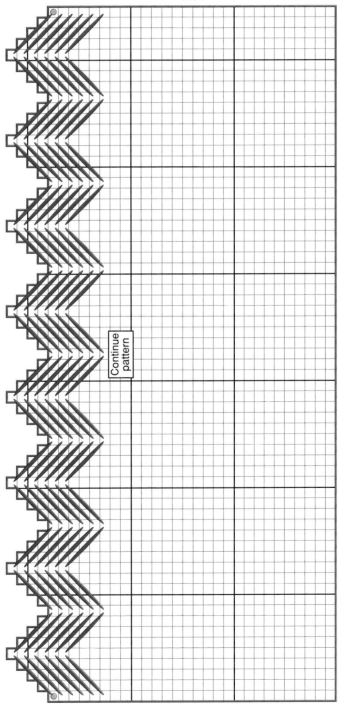

Continue pattern

step 8 and keeping raffia cord up against fence front, glue sign to fence bottom, covering 1" of fence and raffia. Cut tops of loops.

6. Glue large stems to large and medium pumpkins and small stems to small pumpkins, turning some stems left and some right. Glue pumpkins to fence and sign, trimming raffia cord as needed.

7. Coil wire around dowel. Remove wire and stretch. Thread ends through holes indicated on fence graph; bend ends to secure.

8. Cut two 13" lengths of raffia cord and tie in bows to wires at fence corners; glue to secure. ❖

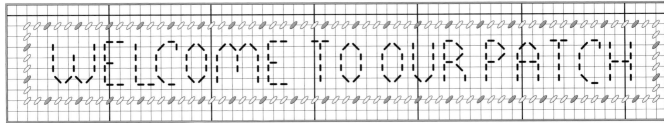

Pumpkin Patch Sign
65 holes x 11 holes
Cut 1

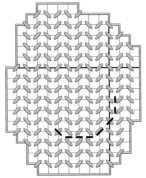

Large Pumpkin
13 holes x 16 holes
Cut 2, reverse 1

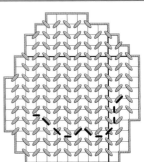

Medium Pumpkin
13 holes x 14 holes
Cut 3, reverse 1

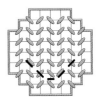

Small Pumpkin
8 holes x 8 holes
Cut 3

COLOR KEY	
Worsted Weight Yarn	**Yards**
■ Tangerine #253	15
■ Mid brown #339	21
□ Honey gold #645	2
■ Paddy green #686	3
Uncoded areas are eggshell #111 Continental Stitches	7
#3 Pearl Cotton	
╱ Black #310 Backstitch	3
● Attach wire for hanging	

Color numbers given are for Red Heart Classic worsted weight yarn Art. E267 and DMC #3 pearl cotton.

Witch's Brew Centerpiece

Continued from page 99

indicated on graph. Glue goblin to inside of base at opening along base top, pushing up base top so eyes peek out.

6. Place stuffing pellets in plastic sandwich bag and tape closed. Place bag inside base. With nickel, Whipstitch bottom edge of base side to base bottom. Glue felt circle to bottom of base.

7. Using photo as a guide, glue one spider to base side, crawling toward peeking goblin. Glue

pumpkin buttons around outside edge of base side as shown or as desired.

Final Assembly

1. Use photo as a guide throughout final assembly. With sewing needle and off-white thread, sew one ghost button to inside front of one of cat's legs, making sure bottom edges are even. Sew remaining ghost button to back of witch's body along bottom

edge, making sure bottom edges are even.

2. Glue witch, cauldron and black cat to base top, gluing cauldron broomstick to back of witch's hands. Glue one spider to crown of witch's hat. Glue remaining spiders to base as desired.

3. Insert battery-operated candle into top of witch's hat. ❖

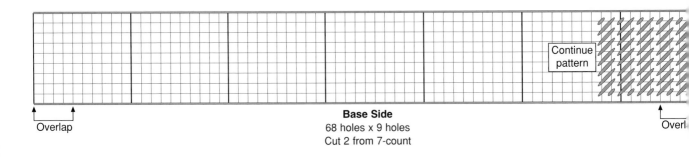

Base Side
68 holes x 9 holes
Cut 2 from 7-count

Overlap

Overl

Mini Candy Bag

Design by Celia Lange Designs

This mini treat bag makes a great party favor or door prize for Halloweeners of all ages!

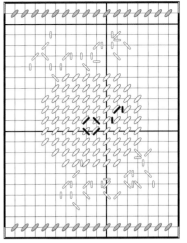

Candy Bag Front & Back
17 holes x 22 holes
Cut 2

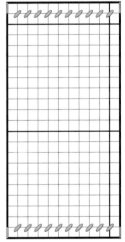

Candy Bag Side
11 holes x 22 holes
Cut 2

Skill Level: Beginner

Materials

- ½ sheet 7-count plastic canvas
- Darice Nylon Plus plastic canvas yarn as listed in color key
- DMC #3 pearl cotton as listed in color key
- Darice straw satin raffia cord:
  ½ yard black #3401-12
  ½ yard orange #3401-20
- Mini ghost decoration
- Hot-glue gun

Instructions

1. Cut plastic canvas according to graphs.

2. Continental Stitch pieces following graphs. Work pearl cotton embroidery over completed background stitching.

3. Overcast handle and top edges of front, back and sides with black. Whipstitch front,

back and sides together with adjacent colors, then Whipstitch front, back and sides to bottom with black.

4. Using photo as a guide throughout, glue handle inside bag sides. Tie a bow with black and orange raffia cord and glue to one side of handle. Glue ghost to bag front. ❖

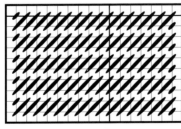

Candy Bag Bottom
17 holes x 11 holes
Cut 1

COLOR KEY	
Plastic Canvas Yarn	**Yards**
■ Black #02	15
▨ Bittersweet #18	5
□ Yellow #26	3
Uncoded areas are black #02 Continental Stitches	
#3 Pearl Cotton	
⁄ White Backstitch	2
✦ Black #310 Backstitch	1
Color numbers given are for Darice Nylon Plus plastic canvas yarn and DMC #3 pearl cotton.	

Candy Bag Handle
41 holes x 4 holes
Cut 1

Halloween
GRAVEYARD

Design by Celia Lange Designs

The creepy characters of October 31 appear on this fun-to-stitch project. Use it to decorate your front door, or prop it against a basket of treats for a table centerpiece.

Skill Level: Intermediate

Materials

- 2 sheets Darice Ultra Stiff 7-count plastic canvas
- Small amount 7-count black plastic canvas
- Red Heart Classic worsted weight yarn Art. E267 as listed in color key
- Red Heart Super Saver worsted weight yarn Art. E301 as listed in color key
- DMC #3 pearl cotton as listed in color key
- Cardboard
- 6" ¼"-wide orange satin ribbon
- Craft stick
- 2 (4mm) movable eyes
- 2 (15mm) movable eyes
- 6" 20-gauge white wrapped florist wire
- Hot-glue gun

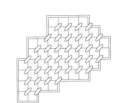

Graveyard Ghost Hand
9 holes x 8 holes
Cut 1

Instructions

1. Cut plastic canvas according to graphs (also see page 106); cut bug legs from black canvas, cutting away blue lines, leaving black lines only. Cut cardboard slightly smaller than gravestone.

2. Stitch pieces following graphs, Continental Stitching and Overcasting uncoded area on boo sign with warm brown and sign on hand sign with Aran.

3. Backstitch ghost's mouth and letters on signs when background stitching is completed. Overcast pieces following graphs.

4. Coil florist wire around pencil. Remove pencil and stretch coil. Using photo as a guide through step 7, thread one end of wire behind gravestone on upper right side. Thread remaining end behind bat. Glue ends to secure. Glue 4mm movable eyes to bat's head. Glue cardboard to backside of gravestone.

5. Glue bug body to bug legs and cap to center top of jack-o'-lantern. Glue 15mm movable eyes to ghost's head. Glue boo sign to one end of craft stick. Tie orange ribbon in a bow, trimming ends as desired, and glue to craft stick just below sign.

6. Glue ghost behind gravestone, ghost's hand to upper left side of gravestone, and boo sign behind ghost's attached hand and behind ghost's head.

7. Glue bug, hand sign and jack-o'-lantern to bottom front of sign. Hang as desired. ❖

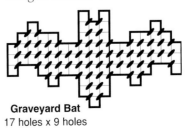

Graveyard Bat
17 holes x 9 holes
Cut 1

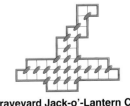

Graveyard Jack-o'-Lantern Cap
10 holes x 8 holes
Cut 1

COLOR KEY

Worsted Weight Yarn	Yards
☐ Yellow #230	1
▨ Orange #245	8
◼ Tangerine #253	3
☐ White #311	20
◼ Black #312	10
☐ Buff #334	1
▨ Mid brown #339	2
☐ Light gray #341	25
▨ Nickel #401	10
▨ Paddy green #686	
Uncoded area on hand sign is Aran #313 Continental Stitches	3
Uncoded area on boo sign is warm brown #336 Continental Stitches	5
⁄ Aran #313 Overcasting	
⁄ Warm brown #336 Overcasting	

#3 Pearl Cotton

	Yards
⁄ Black #310 Backstitch	2
● Black #310 French Knot	
⁄ Ultra very dark desert sand #632 Backstitch	1

Color numbers given are for Red Heart Classic worsted weight yarn Art. E267, Red Heart Super Saver worsted weight yarn Art. E301 and DMC #3 pearl cotton.

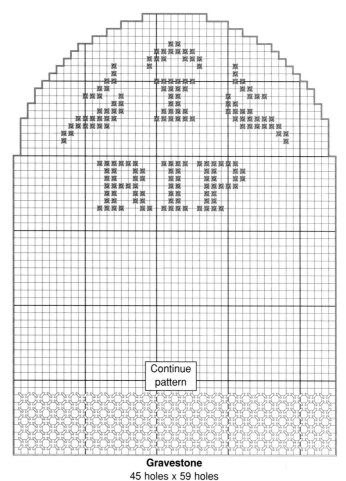

Gravestone
45 holes x 59 holes
Cut 1

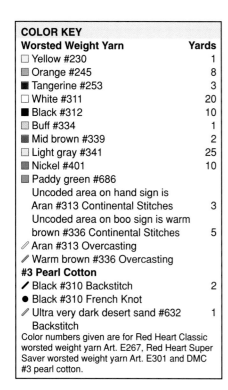

Graveyard Ghost
37 holes x 44 holes
Cut 1

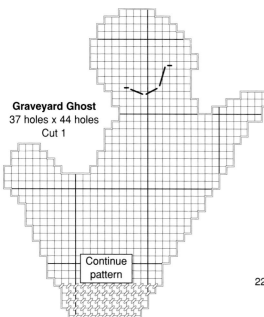

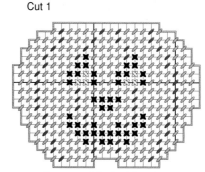

Graveyard Bug
6 holes x 10 holes
Cut 1

Graveyard Jack-o'-Lantern
23 holes x 17 holes
Cut 1

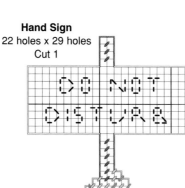

Hand Sign
22 holes x 29 holes
Cut 1

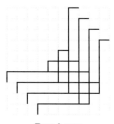

Bug Legs
10 holes x 10 holes
Cut 1
Cut away blue lines,
leaving black lines only
Do not stitch

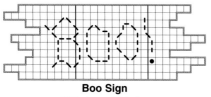

Boo Sign
28 holes x 10 holes
Cut 1

Best Witches

Design by Vicki Blizzard

If you prefer friendly spooks over scary spooks, then these cheery bears wishing you and yours a Happy Halloween are just for you!

Skill Level: Intermediate

Materials

- 1½ sheets Uniek Quick-Count clear 7-count plastic canvas
- ¼ sheet Uniek Quick-Count black 7-count plastic canvas
- Spinrite plastic canvas yarn as listed in color key
- DMC #3 pearl cotton as listed in color key
- DMC 6-strand embroidery floss as listed in color key
- #16 tapestry needle
- 3 (4mm) round black cabochons from The Beadery
- 6 (6mm) round black cabochons from The Beadery
- 6" ⅛"-wide purple satin ribbon
- 6" ⅛"-wide black satin ribbon
- 2 yards ⅛"-wide green satin ribbon
- 24" ¼"-wide orange satin ribbon
- Sheet orange felt
- Hot-glue gun

Cutting & Stitching

1. Cut pumpkins, hats, muzzles, faces, ears, bodies, arms and signs from clear plastic canvas according to graphs (pages 108 and 109). Cut orange felt slightly smaller than each pumpkin.

2. Cut cat, pumpkin eyes, pumpkin mouth and spider from black plastic canvas according to graphs. Cut away shaded gray areas around spider body, leaving black bars for spider's legs.

3. Stitch and Overcast faces, muzzles, ears, signs, cat, spider and pumpkin mouth and eyes following graphs. Work embroidery over completed background stitching.

4. Stitch and Overcast pumpkins

following graphs. Using photo as a guide, work white floss spiderweb on one pumpkin only, stitching five long spokes first. Bring floss up at one hole indicated with red dot. Wrap floss around all five spokes, then bring floss down at hole indicated with red heart. Repeat two more times, following graph. Glue felt to backs of pumpkins.

5. Stitch hat B following graph. Stitch one hat A following graph. Reverse one hat A and stitch with purple grape. Overcast with adjacent colors.

6. Stitch one body following graph, one with purple grape and one with charcoal. Overcast with adjacent colors.

7. Stitch three pairs of arms, reversing one arm in each pair before stitching. Stitch sleeves on one pair as graphed, sleeves on second pair with purple grape and sleeves on third pair with charcoal. Overcast with adjacent colors.

Assembly

1. Using photo as a guide throughout assembly, glue one face to top front of each body. Glue one muzzle to each face. Glue hat that matches body color to top front of each head. Glue two ears to side of each head directly below hat.

2. Glue one body to center top edge of each pumpkin, gluing charcoal bear to spiderweb pumpkin. Glue matching arms to front of body and pumpkin so hands touch in center. Glue one 4mm cabochon to center top of each muzzle for nose. Glue two 6mm cabochons to each face between hat and muzzle for eyes.

3. Cut orange ribbon into three equal lengths. Tie each in a bow, trimming ends as desired. Center and glue one bow to top of each body directly under chin. Cut a

12" length of green ribbon; tie in a bow around cat's neck.

4. Cut a 6" length of green ribbon, tie in a small bow and trim ends. Glue to right side of purple grape hat. Tie black and purple ribbons in small bows; trim ends. Glue black ribbon to center top of brisk green hat and purple ribbon to left side of charcoal hat.

5. Cut three 8" lengths of green ribbon. Tie a knot in one end of one length. Thread this length from back to front through hole at upper corner of one sign, then from front to back at upper corner on opposite side. Pull ribbon until hanging loop is approximately 4". Tie knot in ribbon against back of sign, trimming end as necessary. Repeat with remaining signs.

6. Place purple grape bear pumpkin on left, charcoal bear pumpkin on right and brisk green bear pumpkin in center. Glue

pumpkins together, placing center pumpkin slightly lower than and in front of end pumpkins.

7. Glue black cat to lower left front of left pumpkin. Glue spider to bottom center of spiderweb. Glue eyes and mouth to front of center pumpkin.

8. Hang one sign over each bear's hands so they read, "BEARY BEST WITCHES FOR A HAPPY HALLOWEEN."

9. Thread remaining green ribbon from back to front through top right hole on left pumpkin; pull ribbon through, tying end in knot on backside. Thread remaining end from front to back through top left hole of right pumpkin. Pull ribbon until hanging loop is desired length. ***Note:*** *Loop on sample is approximately 18" long.* Tie knot in ribbon against back of sign, trimming end as necessary. ❖

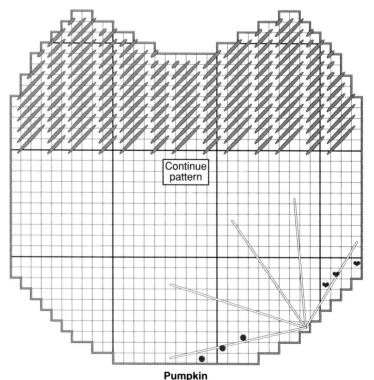

Pumpkin
34 holes x 33 holes
Cut 3 from clear
Stitch spider web on 1 only

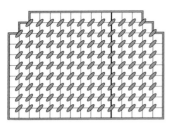

Best Witches Body
15 holes x 10 holes
Cut 3
Stitch 1 as graphed,
1 with purple grape,
1 with charcoal

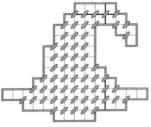

Hat A
14 holes x 11 holes
Cut 2 from clear
Stitch 1 as graphed
Reverse 1, stitch with purple grape

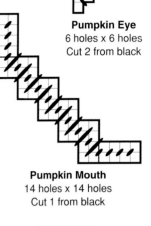

Pumpkin Eye
6 holes x 6 holes
Cut 2 from black

Pumpkin Mouth
14 holes x 14 holes
Cut 1 from black

Ear
3 holes x 3 holes
Cut 6 from clear

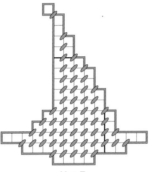

Hat B
14 holes x 15 holes
Cut 1 from clear

Muzzle
7 holes x 4 holes
Cut 3 from clear

COLOR KEY

Plastic Canvas Yarn	Yards
■ Charcoal #0021	8
▨ Brisk green #0027	9
■ Black #0028	8
▨ Orange #0030	36
▨ Walnut #0047	8
☐ Almond #0056	3
Uncoded areas on signs are white #0001 Continental Stitches	9
╱ Purple grape #0024 Overcasting	8
● Black #0028 French Knot	

#3 Pearl Cotton

╱ Very dark mahogany #300 Backstitch	1
╱ Black #310 Backstitch	3

6-Strand Embroidery Floss

╱ White Straight Stitch
Color numbers given are for Spinrite plastic canvas yarn and DMC #3 pearl cotton.

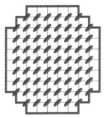

Face
9 holes x 10 holes
Cut 3 from clear

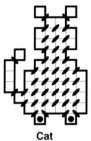

Cat
8 holes x 11 holes
Cut 1 from black

Arm
10 holes x 15 holes
Cut 6 from clear
Stitch 2, reverse 1, as graphed
Stitch 2, reverse 1, replacing
brisk green with purple grape
Stitch 2, reverse 1, replacing
brisk green with charcoal

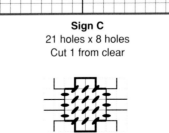

Sign C
21 holes x 8 holes
Cut 1 from clear

Spider
8 holes x 5 holes
Cut 1 from black
Cut away blue lines,
leaving black lines only

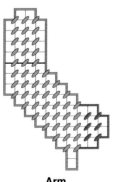

Sign B
14 holes x 7 holes
Cut 1 from clear

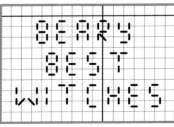

Sign A
17 holes x 11 holes
Cut 1 from clear

TRICK o

Greet trick-or-treaters at your door with this jack-o'-lantern-and-ghost bag filled to the brim with candy treats!

Skill Level: Beginner

Materials

- 3 sheets 7-count plastic canvas
- Uniek Needloft plastic canvas yarn as listed in color key
- #3 pearl cotton as listed in color key
- Hot-glue gun

Instructions

1. Cut plastic canvas according to graphs (below and page 112).

2. Stitch pieces following graphs, working uncoded areas with black yarn Continental Stitches. Stitch embroidery with black pearl cotton when background stitching is completed.

3. Using black yarn throughout, Overcast handle edges and top edges of back, front and sides. Whipstitch front, back and sides together, then Whipstitch front, back and sides to bottom.

4. Using photo as a guide, glue one handle to inside front and one to inside back. ❖

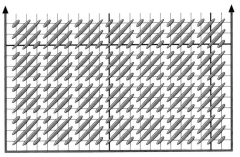

Trick-or-Treat Bag Side
22 holes x 49 holes
Cut 2

Continued on next page

COLOR KEY

Plastic Canvas Yarn	Yards
■ Pumpkin #12	120
■ Mint #24	15
□ White #41	12
Uncoded areas are black #00 Continental Stitches	45
╱ Black #00 Overcasting and Whipstitching	
#3 Pearl Cotton	
╱ Black Backstitch	4
● Black French Knot	

Color numbers given are for Uniek Needloft plastic canvas yarn.

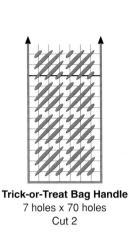

Trick-or-Treat Bag Handle
7 holes x 70 holes
Cut 2

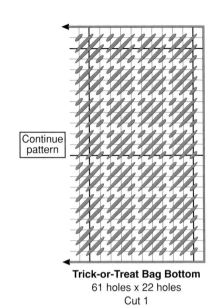

Continue pattern

Trick-or-Treat Bag Bottom
61 holes x 22 holes
Cut 1

Trick-or-Treat Bag Front & Back
61 holes x 49 holes
Cut 2

Halloween Shelf Sitters

Skill Level: Beginner

Materials

- 1½ sheets 7-count plastic canvas
- Spinrite plastic canvas yarn as listed in color key
- Spinrite Bernat Berella "4" worsted weight yarn as listed in color key
- #16 tapestry needle

Instructions

1. Cut three pieces for each character from plastic canvas according to graphs (right and pages 114 and 115).

2. Stitch pieces following graphs. Work black French Knots for cat's eyes. Using daffodil for noses on ghost and cat, work slanted stitches in one direction first, then work slanted stitches in opposite direction on top of first stitches for a padded look. Backstitch mouths on ghost and cat following graphs.

3. Whipstitch seams of each character together with adjacent colors, stitching in each set of holes twice. Overcast remaining edges with adjacent colors.

4. Bend in accordion style to make characters stand. ❖

COLOR KEY

Plastic Canvas Yarn	Yards
☐ Daffodil #0029	1
☐ Apple #0041	1
╱ Daffodil #0029 Backstitch	
Worsted Weight Yarn	
▨ Tangelo #8704	26
▨ Dark lagoon #8822	2
☐ White #8942	22
■ Black #8944	30
╱ Black #8944 Backstitch	
● Black #8944 French Knot	

Color numbers given are for Spinrite plastic canvas yarn and Bernat Berella "4" worsted weight yarn.

Designs by Joan Green

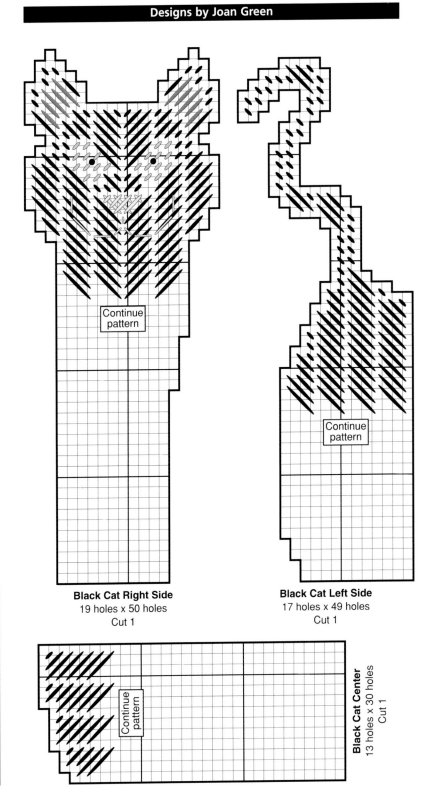

Black Cat Right Side
19 holes x 50 holes
Cut 1

Continue pattern

Black Cat Left Side
17 holes x 49 holes
Cut 1

Continue pattern

Continue pattern

Black Cat Center
13 holes x 30 holes
Cut 1

COLOR KEY

Plastic Canvas Yarn	Yards
☐ Daffodil #0029	1
▨ Apple #0041	1
⟋ Daffodil #0029 Backstitch	
Worsted Weight Yarn	
▨ Tangelo #8704	26
▨ Dark lagoon #8822	2
☐ White #8942	22
■ Black #8944	30
⟋ Black #8944 Backstitch	
● Black #8944 French Knot	

Color numbers given are for Spinrite plastic canvas yarn and Bernat Berella "4" worsted weight yarn.

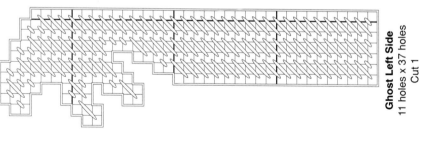

Ghost Left Side
11 holes x 37 holes
Cut 1

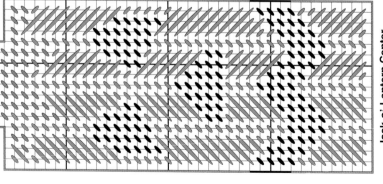

Jack-o'-Lantern Center
16 holes x 43 holes
Cut 1

Set this black cat, ghost and jack-o'-lantern threesome on a shelf or in a window for a unique Halloween decoration. With their folding-style design, they stand on their own.

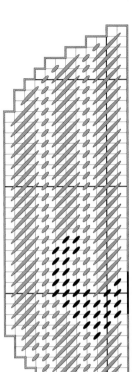

Jack-o'-Lantern Left Side
12 holes x 35 holes
Cut 1

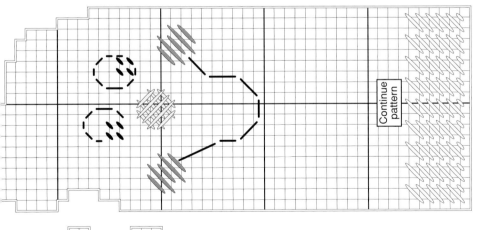

Continue pattern

Ghost Center
19 holes x 48 holes
Cut 1

Ghost Right Side
11 holes x 37 holes
Cut 1

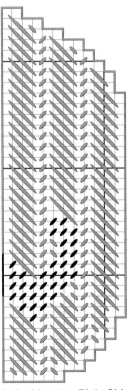

Jack-o'-Lantern Right Side
12 holes x 35 holes
Cut 1

Skill Level: Beginner

Materials
- 1 sheet 7-count plastic canvas
- J. & P. Coats plastic canvas yarn Article E46 as listed in color key
- Anchor 6-strand embroidery floss as listed in color key
- 4 (7mm x 12mm) oval movable eyes
- Tacky craft glue

Instructions

1. Cut plastic canvas according to graphs.

2. Stitch ghost pieces following graph, reversing one ghost before stitching. Work bright Christmas red floss Backstitching for mouth on ghost front only. Whipstitch wrong sides of ghost pieces together along inside and outside edges with white.

3. Stitch bat front following graph, stitching uncoded area with black Continental Stitches. Work bright Christmas red floss Backstitches over completed background stitching.

Spooky
NAPKIN RINGS

Designs by Nancy Marshall

These friendly ghost and bat napkin rings will add colorful fun to all the festivities on Halloween night! Stitch one for everyone at your buffet table!

4. Stitch bat back same as bat front, working entire center area with black Continental Stitches only, eliminating lily pink for ears and bright Christmas red floss Backstitching for mouth. Whipstitch wrong sides of front and back together along inside and outside edges with black.

5. Using photo as a guide, glue movable eyes in place. ◆

COLOR KEY	
Plastic Canvas Yarn	**Yards**
☐ White #01	10
■ Black #12	13
☐ Lily pink #719	1
Uncoded areas on bat are black #12 Continental Stitches	
╱ White #01 Straight Stitch	
╱ Black #12 Straight Stitch	
6-Strand Embroidery Floss	
╱ Bright Christmas red #46 Backstitch	½
Color numbers given are for J. & P. Coats plastic canvas yarn Article E46 and Anchor 6-strand embroidery floss.	

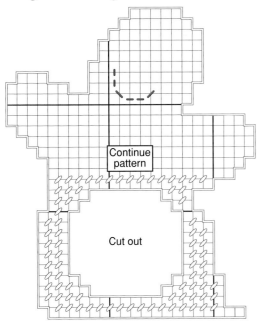

Spooky Ghost
24 holes x 29 holes
Cut 2, reverse 1

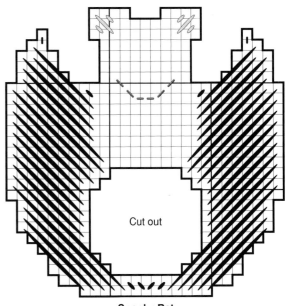

Spooky Bat
27 holes x 27 holes
Cut 2

A Day of Thanks

Harvest a bountiful crop of festive autumn projects just in time for Thanksgiving! Attractive centerpieces, a welcome wreath, nut baskets and other handsome projects will make the day one on which to be extra-thankful!

Thanksgiving Angel

Design by Vicki Blizzard • Shown on page 119

Hang this enchanting angel in your home to remind you and your family to give thanks on Thanksgiving Day and throughout the year.

Skill Level: Advanced

Materials

- 2 sheets clear 7-count plastic canvas
- Small amount tan 7-count plastic canvas
- Red Heart Classic worsted weight yarn Art. E267 as listed in color key
- Red Heart Super Saver worsted weight yarn Art. E301 as listed in color key
- Anchor #3 pearl cotton as listed in color key
- Kreinik ⅛" Ribbon as listed in color key
- 26 (3mm) gold beads by The Beadery
- 2 (5mm) black round cabochons
- Autumn brown mini-curl doll hair by One & Only Creations
- 6" ⅛"-wide ivory satin ribbon
- 15" ¼"-wide ivory satin ribbon
- Polyester fiberfill
- Clear thread and sewing needle
- Hot-glue gun or craft glue

Cutting & Stitching

1. Cut apple and pumpkin from tan plastic canvas and remaining pieces from clear plastic canvas according to graphs (pages 121 and 122). Cut away blue lines at stem areas of pumpkin and apple, leaving black lines only for stems.

2. Stitch and Overcast letters and halo following graphs. Stitch remaining pieces following graphs, reversing two arms and two wings before stitching. Work uncoded areas on arms, dress front, dress back, arches and wheat motifs with light sage Continental Stitches.

3. When background stitching is completed, work French Knots on grapes and nose with 4 plies yarn; work Straight Stitches on dress front and wheat motifs with 2 plies cornmeal yarn; work mouth with Christmas red pearl cotton.

4. Attach beads where indicated on dress front and wheat motifs with clear thread and sewing needle. Glue black cabochons for eyes in place on head front.

5. Overcast apple, grapes, grape leaf, pumpkin and basket with adjacent colors. Do not Overcast stem on apple or pumpkin.

6. With wrong sides together and matching edges, Whipstitch two wing pieces together with off-white. Repeat with second pair of wings. With wrong sides together and matching edges, Whipstitch two arms together with adjacent colors. Repeat with remaining arm pieces.

7. Whipstitch wrong sides of two arch pieces together with cornmeal. Repeat for remaining arch pieces. Whipstitch wrong sides of two wheat motif pieces together with light sage. Repeat with remaining motif pieces.

8. Whipstitch wrong sides of body front and back together with adjacent colors, stuffing body and head firmly with fiberfill before closing.

Assembly

1. Using photo as a guide throughout assembly, tie ⅛" ivory satin ribbon in a small bow; trim ends. Glue bow to body front at neck. Wrap ¼" ivory satin ribbon around waist and tie in a bow at back. Twist ends to curl ribbon and glue to back of dress.

2. Glue wings to angel back and arms to angel front at shoulders. Glue pumpkin and apple to basket back. Glue grape leaf to top front of grapes. Glue grapes to basket front. Glue basket to angel's hands and body front. Glue doll hair to angel's head, following manufacturer's directions, then glue halo to top back of angel's head. Glue letters to arches so top arch reads "LET US" and bottom arch reads "GIVE THANKS".

3. Thread sewing needle with clear thread; bring needle through top center hole of angel's head and through hole indicated on arch with blue dot. Pull thread so there is approximately 1½" of space between head and arch, tie ends in a knot and cut off tails.

4. With clear thread and sewing needle, attach top of one motif to each end of top arch through holes indicated with red dots, so motifs hang ½" below arch. Repeat process, attaching bottom of motifs to bottom arch.

5. Thread an 18" length of gold ⅛" ribbon from back to front where indicated with black dots on arch graph; tie in a double-knot bow at top of arch. Bring ends up and tie in a knot to form a loop for hanging. ❖

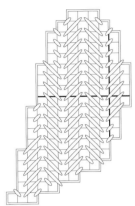

Angel Wing
12 holes x 18 holes
Cut 4, reverse 2, from clear

Angel Arm
12 holes x 9 holes
Cut 4, reverse 2, from clear

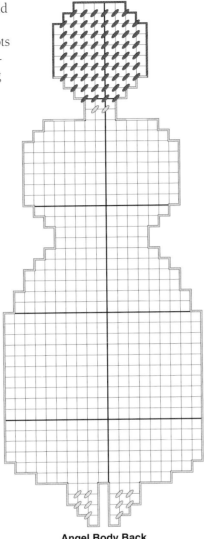

Angel Body Back
19 holes x 49 holes
Cut 1 from clear

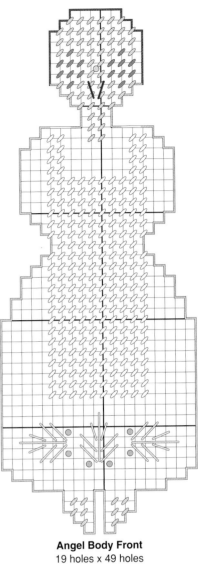

Angel Body Front
19 holes x 49 holes
Cut 1 from clear

Thanksgiving Angel Letters
Cut from clear

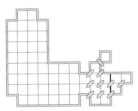

5 holes x 7 holes
Cut 1

5 holes x 7 holes
Cut 2

5 holes x 7 holes
Cut 2

5 holes x 7 holes
Cut 1

5 holes x 7 holes
Cut 2

5 holes x 7 holes
Cut 1

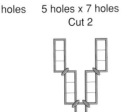

1 hole x 7 holes
Cut 1

5 holes x 7 holes
Cut 1

5 holes x 7 holes
Cut 1

5 holes x 7 holes
Cut 1

5 holes x 7 holes
Cut 1

5 holes x 7 holes
Cut 1

COLOR KEY

Worsted Weight Yarn	Yards
□ Off-white #3	15
□ Cornmeal #220	45
■ Orange #245	1
■ Sea coral #246	1
□ Peach #325	6
■ Mid brown #339	2
■ Purple #596	1
■ Dark sage #633	8
■ Cherry red #912	1
Uncoded areas are light sage #631 Continental Stitches	45
⁄ Light sage #631 Whipstitching	
⁄ Cornmeal #220 Straight Stitch	
○ Peach #325 French Knot	
● Purple #596 French Knot	
⅛" Ribbon	
■ Gold #002HL	1
#3 Pearl Cotton	
⁄ Christmas red #47 Straight Stitch	⅙
○ Attach gold bead	

Color numbers given are for Red Heart Classic worsted weight yarn Art. E267, Red Heart Super Saver worsted weight yarn Art. E301, Kreinik ⅛" Ribbon and Anchor #3 pearl cotton by Coats & Clark.

Grape Leaf
2 holes x 2 holes
Cut 1 from clear

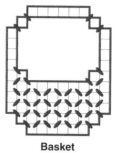

Basket
10 holes x 12 holes
Cut 1 from clear

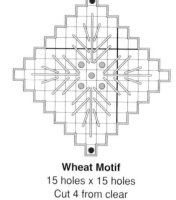

Wheat Motif
15 holes x 15 holes
Cut 4 from clear

Grapes
3 holes x 4 holes
Cut 1 from clear

Apple
4 holes x 6 holes
Cut 1 from tan
Cut away blue
lines at stem

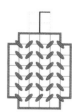

Pumpkin
6 holes x 9 holes
Cut 1 from tan
Cut away blue
lines at stem

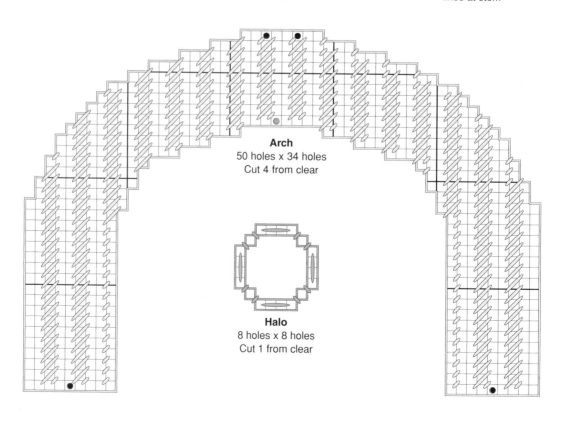

Arch
50 holes x 34 holes
Cut 4 from clear

Halo
8 holes x 8 holes
Cut 1 from clear

Autumn Florals

C E N T E R P I E C E

Design by Celia Lange Designs

Dress up your Thanksgiving dinner table or buffet with this lovely floral centerpiece. Beautiful silk or dried flowers make this arrangement one you'll use year after year.

Skill Level: Beginner

Materials

- 1 sheet 7-count plastic canvas
- 6" plastic canvas radial circle
- Darice Nylon Plus plastic canvas yarn as listed in color key
- Darice straw satin raffia cord: 14 yards Christmas green #3401-19
- Assorted autumn silk flowers, picks, pods and leaves
- Floral foam
- Tissue paper
- Hot-glue gun

Instructions

1. Cut plastic canvas according to graphs.

2. Stitch vase bottom, sides and corner pieces following graphs. Work Backstitches when background stitching is completed.

3. Using bittersweet throughout, Overcast top edges of sides and corners. Whipstitch sides to corners, easing as necessary to fit. Whipstitch sides and corners to bottom.

4. Using green raffia cord through step 5, for base, Straight Stitch around circle from the center row of holes over two bars to the third row of holes.

5. Continue Straight Stitching around circle from the third row of holes to the seventh row, from the seventh to the 13th and from the 13th to the 19th, which is the outside row of holes, using two stitches per hole as necessary to cover canvas. Overcast edge.

6. Center and glue vase to base. Cut floral foam to fit; glue inside vase. Stuff tissue paper around floral foam to keep vase shape. Arrange flowers, pods and leaves in floral foam as desired, reserving and gluing several to base. ❖

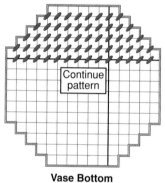

Vase Bottom
15 holes x 15 holes
Cut 1

COLOR KEY

Plastic Canvas Yarn	Yards
■ Sundown #16	21
▨ Bittersweet #18	50
╱ Sundown #16 Backstitch	

Color numbers given are for Darice Nylon Plus plastic canvas yarn.

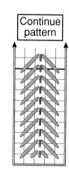

Vase Corner
5 holes x 29 holes
Cut 4

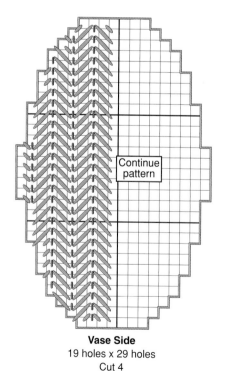

Vase Side
19 holes x 29 holes
Cut 4

Pinecone Welcome
W R E A T H

Design by Carol Nartowicz

*Welcome guests into your home throughout the autumn season
with this handsome pinecone and foliage welcome wreath.*

Skill Level: Advanced

Materials

- 1 sheet ivory 7-count plastic canvas
- 2 sheets Darice clear 7-count Super Soft plastic canvas
- Uniek Needloft plastic canvas yarn as listed in color key
- Fusible fleece
- Hot-glue gun

Wreath & Letters

1. Cut one wreath from ivory plastic canvas; cut one wreath and letters from soft plastic canvas according to graphs. Wreath pieces will remain unstitched.

2. Using wreath as a template, cut fleece to fit. Place fleece between two wreath pieces and Whipstitch together along inside and outside edges with eggshell.

3. Stitch and Overcast letters with burgundy. *Note: The letter "W" is also the letter "M" turned upside down.*

Leaves

1. Cut six leaves from soft plastic canvas according to graph.

2. Stitch leaves following graphs, stitching two as graphed, two with burgundy, one with gold and one with maple. Overcast with adjacent colors.

Pinecones

1. Cut pinecone pieces from soft plastic canvas according

to graphs. Half pinecone backs will remain unstitched.

2. Using cinnamon through step 5, Continental and Long Stitch pieces following graphs, overlapping four holes on whole pinecones before stitching.

3. For whole pinecones, Overcast top spokes, then pull together along inside top edges with a gathering stitch; secure inside. Whipstitch bottom spokes together. Overcast whole pinecone scales.

4. Using photo as a guide, wrap and glue three scales around each whole pinecone, overlapping and spacing evenly.

5. For half pinecones, Whipstitch side edges to back from dot to dot. Overcast and gather top spokes following step 3 for whole pinecones; Whipstitch bottom spokes together.

6. Using photo as a guide, wrap and glue three scales around front of each half pinecone, overlapping and spacing evenly.

Assembly

1. Using photo as a guide, glue letters to top of wreath. Glue leaves and pinecones to bottom of wreath.

2. Hang as desired. ❖

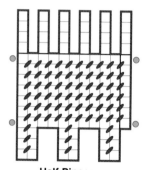

Half Pinecone
11 holes x 14 holes
Cut 2 from soft

COLOR KEY	
Plastic Canvas Yarn	**Yards**
■ Burgundy #03	12
■ Pumpkin #12	8
Maple #13	4
■ Cinnamon #14	45
Gold #17	4
⁄ Eggshell #39 Whipstitching	6
Color numbers given are for Uniek Needloft plastic canvas yarn.	

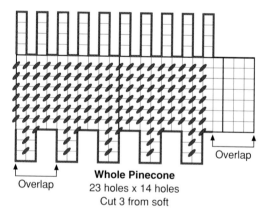

Overlap

Overlap

Whole Pinecone
23 holes x 14 holes
Cut 3 from soft

Wreath Letters
8 holes x 10 holes

Half Pinecone Back
8 holes x 7 holes
Cut 2 from soft
Do not stitch

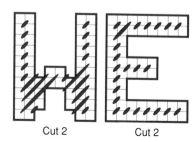

Cut 2

Cut 2

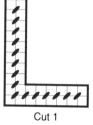

Cut 1

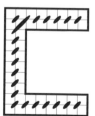

Cut 1

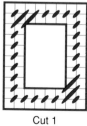

Cut 1

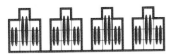

Half Pinecone Scales
15 holes x 4 holes
Cut 6 from soft

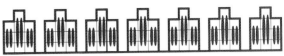

Whole Pinecone Scales
27 holes x 4 holes
Cut 9 from soft

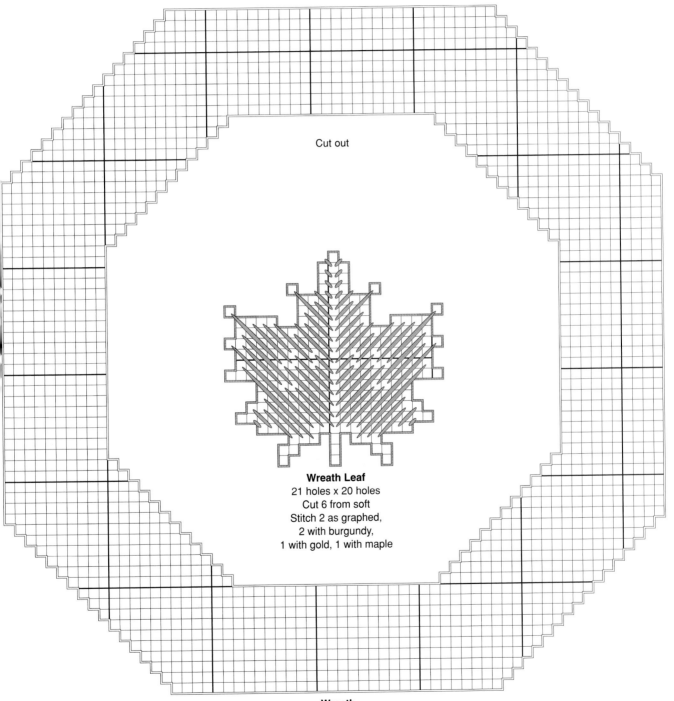

Cut out

Wreath Leaf
21 holes x 20 holes
Cut 6 from soft
Stitch 2 as graphed,
2 with burgundy,
1 with gold, 1 with maple

Wreath
64 holes x 64 holes
Cut 1 from ivory
Cut 1 from soft
Do not stitch

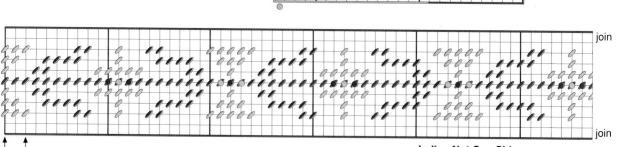

Indian Nut Cup Feather
7 holes x 29 holes
Cut 2, reverse 1

join

join

Overlap

Indian Nut Cup Side
90 holes x 10 holes
Cut 1

Indian Nut Cup

Design by Celia Lange Designs

Skill Level: Beginner

Materials

- ½ sheet 7-count plastic canvas
- 6" plastic canvas radial circle
- Darice Nylon Plus plastic canvas yarn as listed in color key
- 11 (size 6/0 or E) dark red giant seed beads
- 10 (size 6/0 or E) green giant seed beads
- Sewing needle and thread to match bead colors
- Hot-glue gun

Instructions

1. Cut plastic canvas according to graphs. For nut cup bottom, cut the five outermost rows of holes from 6" radial circle so there are 14 rows of holes, including the center holes.

2. Stitch pieces following graphs, reversing one feather before stitching and overlapping two holes on side as indicated before stitching. Continental Stitch uncoded areas with beige. Attach seed beads to side where indicated on graph using sewing needle and matching thread.

3. Using beige throughout, Straight Stitch around circle from the center row of holes over two bars to the third row of holes. Continue Straight Stitching around circle from the third row of holes to the fifth row, from the fifth to the eighth, from the eighth to the 11th and from the 11th to the 14th, which is the outside row of holes, using two stitches per hole as necessary to cover canvas.

4. Whipstitch wrong sides of feathers together from dot to dot down and around center spine following graph. Overcast remaining edges with rust.

5. With brown, Overcast top edge of side, then Whipstitch bottom edge to circle. Using photo as a guide, glue feather to seam of cup side.

Turkey Nut Cup

Design by Nancy Marshall

Skill Level: Beginner

Materials

- ½ sheet 7-count plastic canvas
- Darice Nylon Plus plastic canvas yarn as listed in color key.
- Brown and tan felt
- Craft glue

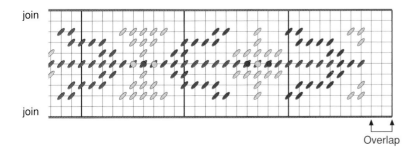

join

join

Overlap

COLOR KEY	
INDIAN NUT CUP	
Plastic Canvas Yarn	**Yards**
▦ Brown #36	4
▢ Rust #51	5
■ Crimson #53	3
▢ Fern #57	2
Uncoded areas are beige #43 Continental Stitches	2
● Attach dark red seed bead	
○ Attach green seed bead	
Color numbers given are for Darice Nylon Plus plastic canvas yarn.	

Instructions

1. Cut plastic canvas according to graphs. Cut two 12-hole x 16-hole pieces for cup sides and one 12-hole x 12-hole piece for cup bottom. Using front and back as templates, cut tan felt to fit front and brown felt to fit back.

2. Continental Stitch sides and bottom with maple. Stitch cup front, back and wings following graphs, working uncoded areas with sundown Continental Stitches.

3. With maple, Whipstitch sides to front and back from dot to dot, then Whipstitch front, back and sides to bottom. Overcast remaining cup edges and wings with adjacent colors.

4. Glue felt to wrong sides of front and back. Glue wings at an angle to sides, making sure bottom edges are even. ❖

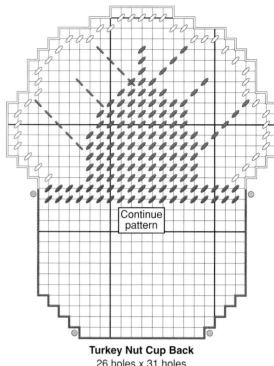

Turkey Nut Cup Back
26 holes x 31 holes
Cut 1

COLOR KEY
TURKEY NUT CUP

Plastic Canvas Yarn	Yards
■ Black #02	1
▨ Tangerine #15	1
■ Christmas red #19	1
□ Eggshell #24	2
▨ Maple #35	13
▨ Brown #36	5
▨ Sandstone #47	5
Uncoded areas are sundown #16 Continental Stitches	4
⁄ Sundown #16 Overcasting	
⁄ Brown #36 Backstitch	

Color numbers given are for Darice Nylon Plus plastic canvas yarn.

Turkey Nut Cup Front
20 holes x 28 holes
Cut 1

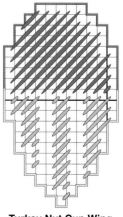

Turkey Nut Cup Wing
11 holes x 19 holes
Cut 2

HARVESTTIME
Bread Basket

Design by Robin Howard-Will

Filled with fresh-from-the-oven rolls, this checkerboard-and-turkey bread basket is both useful and decorative!

Skill Level: Beginner

Materials

- 3 sheets 7-count plastic canvas
- Darice Nylon Plus plastic canvas yarn as listed in color key
- 4 (5mm) movable eyes
- Hot-glue gun or craft glue

Instructions

1. Cut plastic canvas according to graphs.

2. Stitch pieces following graphs, reversing two wings before stitching. Basket bottom will remain unstitched.

3. Using maple throughout, Whipstitch short edges of basket sides together, then Whipstitch bottom to sides, placing seams at the center of long straight sides. Overcast long edges of handle. Center short edges of handle over seams and Whipstitch to top edge of basket, Overcasting top edge while Whipstitching.

4. Overcast tail feathers and wings with brown. Overcast turkey legs and feet with yellow and remaining edges with brown. Using yellow and with wrong sides together, Whipstitch straight edges of two beak pieces together; Overcast remaining edges. Repeat with remaining two beak pieces.

5. Using photo as a guide throughout, center and glue tail feathers over basket seams. Glue turkeys to centers of tail feathers. Glue eyes to turkey heads where indicated on graph. Center and glue beaks to bars above red wattle. Glue one pair of wings to each turkey body. ❖

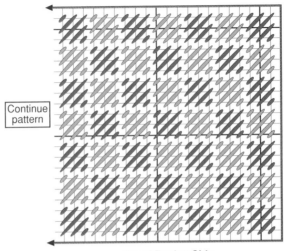

Bread Basket Side
88 holes x 22 holes
Cut 2

COLOR KEY	
Plastic Canvas Yarn	**Yards**
▨ Tangerine #15	32
▨ Burnt orange #17	8
■ Cinnamon #20	1
☐ Yellow #26	10
▨ Maple #35	38
■ Brown #36	4
● Attach eye	
Color numbers given are for Darice Nylon Plus plastic canvas yarn.	

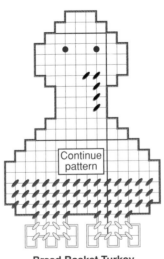

Bread Basket Turkey
15 holes x 22 holes
Cut 2

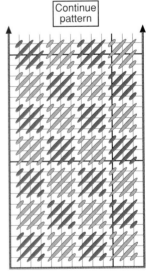

Bread Basket Handle
13 holes x 88 holes
Cut 1

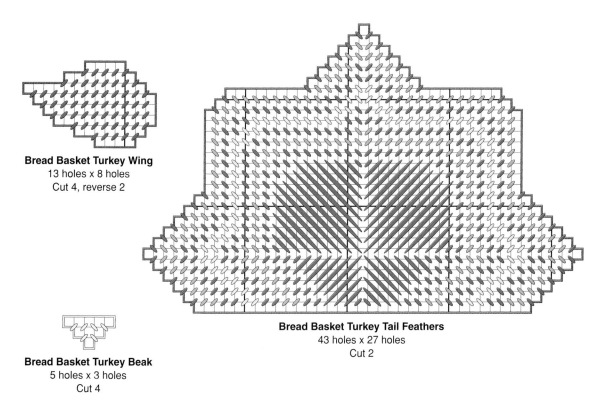

Bread Basket Turkey Wing
13 holes x 8 holes
Cut 4, reverse 2

Bread Basket Turkey Tail Feathers
43 holes x 27 holes
Cut 2

Bread Basket Turkey Beak
5 holes x 3 holes
Cut 4

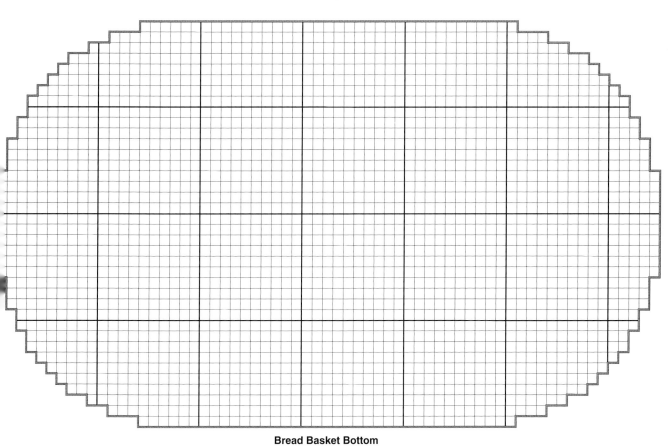

Bread Basket Bottom
65 holes x 38 holes
Cut 1

SCARECROW
Centerpiece

Design by Carol Nartowicz

This cheery scarecrow surely won't frighten any of your guests away!
Surrounded by hay bales and pumpkins, he makes a delightful centerpiece!

Skill Level: Intermediate

Materials

- 1 sheet green 7-count plastic canvas
- 1 sheet Darice clear 7-count Ultra Stiff plastic canvas
- 2 sheets Darice clear 7-count Super Soft plastic canvas
- Uniek Needloft plastic canvas yarn as listed in color key
- Darice straw satin raffia cord as listed in color key
- DMC 6-strand embroidery floss as listed in color key
- 8" ¼"-diameter dowel
- Polyester fiberfill
- Glue gun

Base and Dowel Supports

1. Cut two base pieces from green plastic canvas and two from stiff plastic canvas; cut nine dowel supports from green plastic canvas according to graphs (page 137). Base and dowel support pieces will remain unstitched.

2. Using holly throughout, place clear stiff base pieces between green base pieces and Whipstitch together with holly through all four layers.

3. Place nine dowel support pieces together and stitch to base where indicated on graphs.

Scarecrow

1. Cut hat pieces and scarecrow front and back from soft plastic canvas according to graphs (page 136).

2. Stitch pieces following graphs, working uncoded areas on scarecrow shirt with peach Continental Stitches. Work floss Backstitches and Straight Stitches over completed background stitching.

3. With black, Overcast bottom edges of hat pieces; Whipstitch wrong sides of hat front and back together along remaining edges. On scarecrow front and back, Overcast bottom edges from dot to dot with teal, wrist edges from dot to dot with red and side edges of heads from dot to dot with eggshell.

4. Using photo as a guide through step 5, glue several lengths of raffia cord to backside of legs, arms and head on front piece, threading a couple strands raffia to the front on both legs where desired. Whipstitch wrong sides of scarecrow front and back together along remaining edges following graphs. Secure raffia on front of pant legs with a dot of glue.

5. Insert scarecrow head into bottom of hat and glue in place. Glue dowel inside right pant leg, tilting scarecrow slightly to the right. Insert dowel in support on base.

Hay Bales

1. Cut hay bale pieces from stiff plastic canvas according to graphs (pages 136 and 137).

2. Long Stitch hay bale sides and end following graphs. Whipstitch two large sides to two small sides along long edges, then Whipstitch two ends to sides with raffia cord, stuffing with fiberfill before closing. Repeat for second hay bale.

3. Using photo as a guide through step 4, cut raffia into 1" pieces and randomly glue to hay bales. Wrap two lengths of very ultra dark brown floss around each bale, knotting in front; trim ends as desired.

4. Glue one bale to back left corner of base. Glue second bale on top of first bale at an angle.

Pumpkins

1. Cut pumpkin sides and tops from soft plastic canvas following graphs (page 137).

2. Stitch sides and tops following graphs, working a ½" holly Turkey Loop Stitch (Fig. 1, page 136) in center of each top. Overcast tops with holly.

3. Using pumpkin throughout,

**Fig. 1
Turkey Loop Stitch**

Bring needle up at 1, down at 2,
leaving a small loop above intersection.
Anchor loop by coming up behind loop
at 3 and going down at 4.

Whipstitch seven large pumpkin sides together, stuffing
with fiberfill before closing. Repeat with remaining large
pumpkin sides and then with small pumpkin sides.

4. Using photo as a guide throughout, wrap brown
floss around sides of one large and one small pumpkin,
gluing at tops and bottoms to secure. Glue pumpkin
tops to tops of pumpkins, then glue pumpkins to
base around scarecrow. ❖

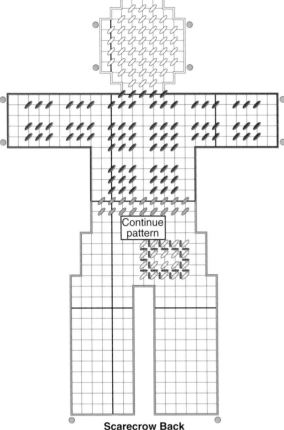

Scarecrow Back
26 holes x 39 holes
Cut 1 from soft

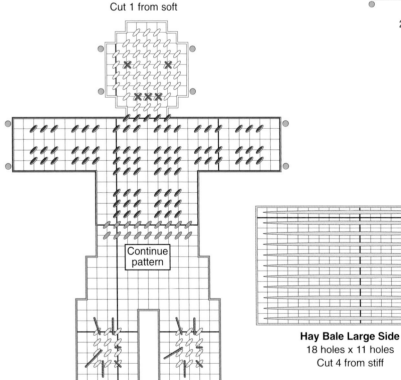

Scarecrow Front
26 holes x 39 holes
Cut 1 from soft

Scarecrow Hat
11 holes x 8 holes
Cut 2 from soft

Hay Bale Large Side
18 holes x 11 holes
Cut 4 from stiff

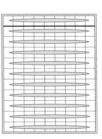

Hay Bale End
9 holes x 11 holes
Cut 4 from stiff

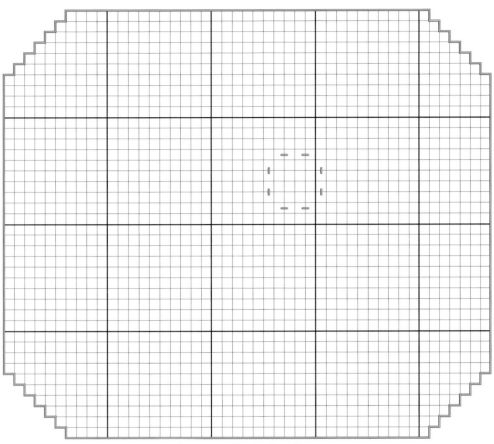

Scarecrow Centerpiece Base
47 holes x 40 holes
Cut 2 from green
Cut 2 from stiff
Do not stitch

Pumpkin Top
6 holes x 6 holes
Cut 3 from soft

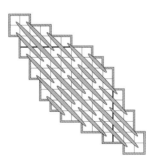

Pumpkin Large Side
13 holes x 13 holes
Cut 14 from soft

Pumpkin Small Side
10 holes x 10 holes
Cut 7 from soft

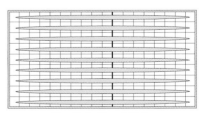

Hay Bale Small Side
18 holes x 9 holes
Cut 4 from stiff

Dowel Support
6 holes x 6 holes
Cut 9 from green
Do not stitch

COLOR KEY	
Plastic Canvas Yarn	**Yards**
■ Red #01	3
■ Black #02	2
▨ Pumpkin #12	21
☐ Straw #19	1
▨ Holly #27	6
☐ Eggshell #39	2
▨ Teal #54	9
Uncoded areas are peach	
#47 Continental Stitches	3
● Holly #27 Turkey Loop	
Straw Satin Raffia Cord	
☐ Tan #3401-08	14
6-Strand Embroidery Floss	
╱ Very ultra dark brown #3371	
Backstitch and Straight Stitch	6
╱ Attach dowel supports to base	
Color numbers given are for Uniek Needloft plastic canvas yarn, Darice straw satin raffia cord and DMC 6-strand embroidery floss.	

Happy Hanukkah

Gold and silver accents make the projects in this chapter sparkle with beauty. From gifts to table decorations, they will make this year's Hanukkah celebration one to be remembered!

Shalom Vase

Whether displayed on your dinner table or on a shelf, this beautiful vase celebrates peace throughout the year.

Design by Celia Lange Designs • Shown on page 139

Skill Level: Beginner

Materials

- 2 sheets 7-count plastic canvas
- Small amount 10-count plastic canvas
- Red Heart Super Saver worsted weight yarn Art. E301 as listed in color key
- Kreinik ⅛" Ribbon as listed in color key
- DMC #3 pearl cotton as listed in color key
- Floral foam
- Assorted silk flowers: blue, white
- Silver pinecones and evergreen
- 10" fine silver-tone jewelry chain
- 2 silver-tone jump rings
- Needle-nose pliers
- Low-temperature glue gun

Instructions

1. Cut vase front, back, sides and bottom from 7-count plastic canvas; cut plaque from 10-count plastic canvas according to graphs (right and page 147).

2. Stitch pieces following graphs, stitching Star of David on vase front only; work back entirely in light periwinkle and periwinkle, following pattern established on vase front. Work Backstitches on plaque and sides when background stitching is completed.

3. Overcast top edges of sides, front and back with silver ribbon. Using periwinkle throughout, Whipstitch sides to front and back, forming vase. Whipstitch vase to bottom.

4. Using needle-nose pliers, thread one jump ring through each top corner of plaque. Thread end of chain on one jump ring; close ring. With plaque at front, wrap chain around neck of vase; cut off extra chain. Thread remaining end of chain on jump ring; close ring.

5. Cut floral foam to fit inside vase; glue to vase bottom. Using photo as a guide, arrange flowers, pinecones and evergreen as desired in foam. ❖

Continued on page 147

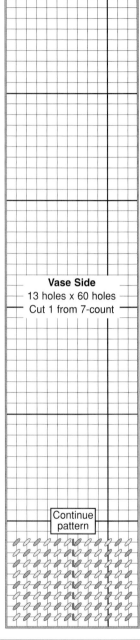

Vase Side
13 holes x 60 holes
Cut 1 from 7-count

Continue pattern

COLOR KEY	
Worsted Weight Yarn	**Yards**
☐ Light periwinkle	45
☐ Periwinkle	50
⅛" **Ribbon**	
☐ Silver #001	8
╱ Silver #001 Backstitch	
#3 Pearl Cotton	
☐ Dark cornflower blue #792	2
Uncoded area on plaque is white Continental Stitches	1
╱ Dark cornflower blue #792 Backstitch	
Color numbers given are for Red Heart Super Saver yarn Art. E301, Kreinik ⅛" Ribbon and DMC #3 pearl cotton.	

STAR OF DAVID

Design by Angie Arickx

Hang this ornament to celebrate your Jewish family's heritage.

Skill Level: Intermediate

Materials

- 5" plastic canvas hexagon by Uniek
- ⅛"-wide Plastic Canvas 7 Metallic Needlepoint Yarn by Rainbow Gallery as listed in color key
- #16 tapestry needle
- Suction cup with hook

Instructions

1. Cut star from hexagon according to graph, cutting away gray areas. Do not trim hanger loop from hexagon.

2. Stitch and Overcast star following graph.

3. Hang as desired, using suction cup and hanger loop. ❖

COLOR KEY	
⅛" Metallic Needlepoint Yarn	**Yards**
☐ Gold #PC7	9
Color number given is for Rainbow Gallery Plastic Canvas 7 Metallic Needlepoint Yarn.	

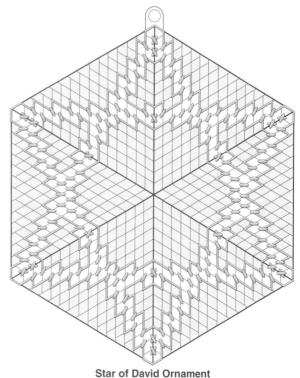

Star of David Ornament
Stitch 1

MENORAH

Design by Angie Arickx

Make a gift to a loved one extra-special by presenting it in this lovely keepsake box adorned with menorahs and a Star of David.

Skill Level: Beginner

Materials

- ½ sheet 7-count plastic canvas
- 2 (5") plastic canvas hexagons by Uniek
- Uniek Needloft plastic canvas yarn as listed in color key
- ⅛"-wide Plastic Canvas 7 Metallic Needlepoint Yarn by Rainbow Gallery as listed in color key
- #16 tapestry needle

Instructions

1. Cut box sides from plastic canvas according to graphs. Cut six 16-hole by 4-hole pieces for lid sides.

2. Stitch three box sides following graph and three with royal Continental Stitches only. Stitch lid top with royal and gold following graph and lid bottom with royal only. Using royal through step 3, Continental Stitch lid sides.

3. Overcast lid edges, top edges of box sides and bottom edges of lid sides. Whipstitch box sides together, then Whipstitch sides to bottom. Whipstitch lid sides together, then center and sew to underside of lid top. ❖

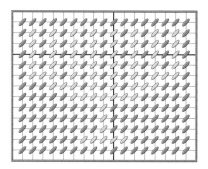

COLOR KEY

Plastic Canvas Yarn	Yards
■ Royal #32	66
╱ Royal #32 Backstitch	
⅛" Metallic Needlepoint Yarn	
☐ Gold #PC7	8

Color numbers given are for Uniek Needloft plastic canvas yarn and Rainbow Gallery Plastic Canvas 7 Metallic Needlepoint Yarn.

Gift Box Side
18 holes x 14 holes
Cut 6
Stitch 3 as graphed
Stitch 3 with royal blue only

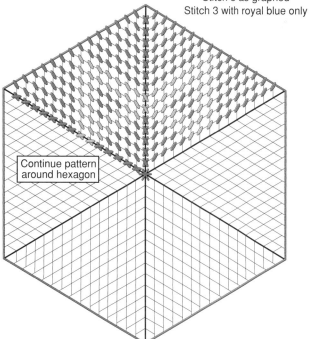

Gift Box Lid Top & Gift Box Bottom
Stitch Lid Top as graphed
Stitch Box Bottom with royal only

Peaceful

DOILY

Add serenity and beauty to your home with this lovely doily accented with doves— a traditional symbol of peace.

Design by Vicki Blizzard

Skill Level: Intermediate

Materials

- 1 sheet Uniek Quick-Count 7-count plastic canvas
- 6 (3") plastic canvas radial circles by Uniek
- 2 (9") plastic canvas radial circles by Uniek
- Uniek Needloft plastic canvas yarn as listed in color key
- Uniek Needloft metallic craft cord as listed in color key
- #16 tapestry needle
- 2 (3mm) round gold beads
- 12" x 18" piece white felt
- Small sharp-pointed scissors
- Sewing needle and clear thread
- Hot-glue gun

Instructions

1. Cut one doily and two doves from plastic canvas according to graphs (pages 146 and 147). Cut two large scallops from 9" circles; cut four medium scallops and two small scallops from 3" circles according to graphs, cutting away gray areas.

2. Stitch pieces following graphs, reversing one dove before stitching. Work tail and beak stitches when background stitching is completed. Overcast base and large scallops with gold cord and white yarn, remaining scallops with gold cord and doves with white yarn.

3. Using sewing needle and clear thread through step 5, attach gold beads where indicated on graph for doves' eyes.

4. Sew large scallops to each end of doily base. Using photo as a guide, sew two medium and one small scallop to each long edge of base, placing small scallop between medium scallops.

5. Sew beak of one dove to one large scallop where indicated on graph with blue dot; sew tail where indicated with red dot. Tack wing to doily base. Repeat with remaining dove on opposite side of doily.

6. Working with small areas at a time, glue uncut felt sheet to back of assembled doily. When doily is completely covered and glue is dry, carefully trim felt from all open areas using small sharp-pointed scissors. ❖

Small Scallop
Cut 2

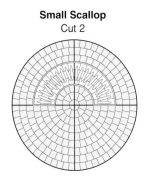

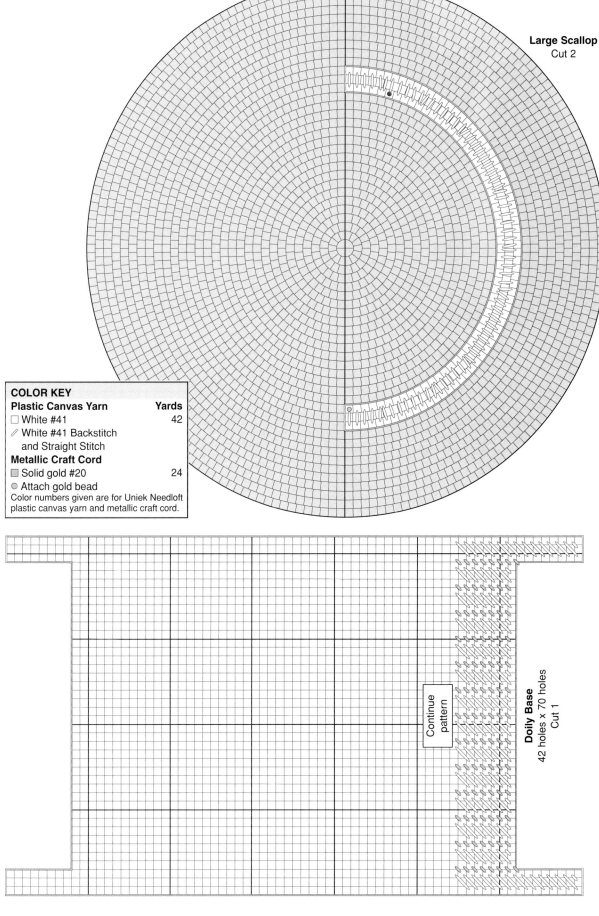

Large Scallop
Cut 2

COLOR KEY

Plastic Canvas Yarn	Yards
☐ White #41	42
⟋ White #41 Backstitch and Straight Stitch	
Metallic Craft Cord	
☐ Solid gold #20	24
⊙ Attach gold bead	

Color numbers given are for Uniek Needloft plastic canvas yarn and metallic craft cord.

Continue pattern

Doily Base
42 holes x 70 holes
Cut 1

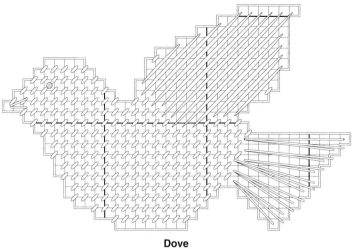

Dove
34 holes x 21 holes
Cut 2, reverse 1

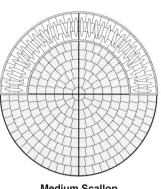

Medium Scallop
Cut 4

Shalom Vase

Continued from page 140

Continue pattern

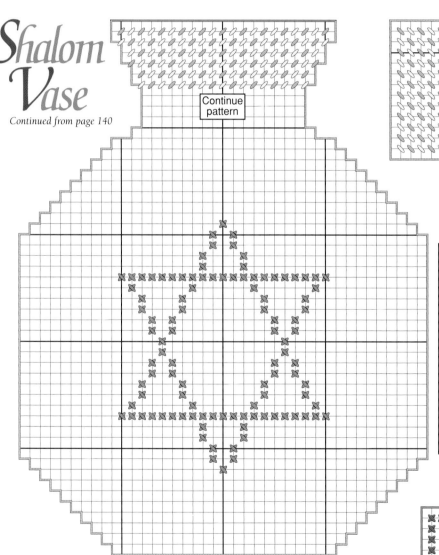

Vase Front & Back
40 holes x 50 holes
Cut 2 from 7-count
Stitch 1 with design
Stitch 1 without design

Vase Bottom
22 holes x 13 holes
Cut 1 from 7-count

COLOR KEY

Worsted Weight Yarn	Yards
☐ Light periwinkle	45
▧ Periwinkle	50

⅛" Ribbon

■ Silver #001	8
╱ Silver #001 Backstitch	

#3 Pearl Cotton

■ Dark cornflower blue #792	2
Uncoded area on plaque is white Continental Stitches	1
╱ Dark cornflower blue #792 Backstitch	

Color numbers given are for Red Heart Super Saver yarn Art. E301, Kreinik ⅛" Ribbon and DMC #3 pearl cotton.

Plaque
19 holes x 7 holes
Cut 1 from 10-count

Merry Christmas

Turn your home into a Christmas wonderland with this collection of enchanting decorations, keepsake gifts and ornaments aplenty! You'll find dozens of great ideas for bringing holiday cheer to your friends and family during this Christmas season!

Mr. & Mrs. SNOWMAN

Designs by Janna Britton • Shown on page 149

These free-standing snowpeople are just what you need to dress up your holiday dining table or mantel top! Surround them with pinecones and holly to make a festive display!

Skill Level: Beginner

Materials

- 1 sheet 7-count plastic canvas
- Uniek Needloft plastic canvas yarn as listed in color key
- Red Heart Super Saver worsted weight yarn Art. E301 as listed in color key
- Honeysuckle Yarns rayon chenille yarn by Ruby Mills as listed in color key
- DMC 6-strand embroidery floss as listed in color key
- DMC 6-strand rayon floss as listed in color key
- ¼"-wide satin ribbon as listed in color key
- #16 tapestry needle
- 2 sheets white felt
- 4 (3¾") wooden doll pins
- ¾" red lacquered apple
- Low-temperature glue gun

Instructions

1. Cut plastic canvas according to graphs.

2. Stitch Mr. Snowman following graph. Overcast edges following graph. When background stitching and Overcasting are completed, Straight Stitch nose with 12 strands bright orange floss, Backstitch between feet with 6 strands black floss, and work black yarn French Knots for eyes and maple yarn Backstitches for mouth.

3. For bow tie, work five red satin ribbon Straight

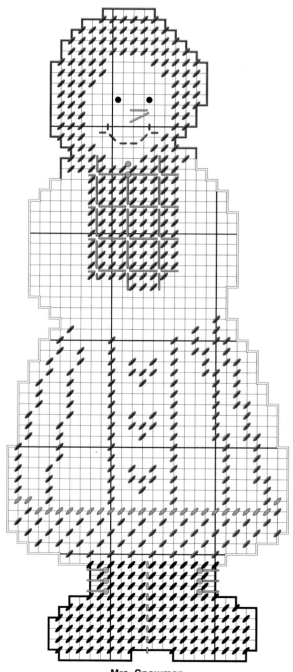

Mrs. Snowman
27 holes x 61 holes
Cut 1

Stitches below chin, then gather all five in the center and work Straight Stitch over all five as indicated.

4. Stitch Mrs. Snowman following graph, using a double strand of Christmas green rayon chenille

yarn on skirt. Overcast edges following graph.

5. When background stitching and Overcasting are completed, work French Knot eyes with black yarn. Backstitch over bodice with 6 strands kelly green rayon floss, stitch embroidery on boots with 6 strands very light gray green, Straight Stitch nose with 12 strands bright orange and Backstitch mouth with 12 strands bright Christmas red.

6. Thread ends of 6" length of red satin ribbon from back to front through holes indicated with blue dots; tie in a bow and trim ends as desired.

7. For Mr. Snowman, glue two doll pins together end to end, then glue to center backside, making sure bottom edges are even. Glue white felt to back of snowman; trim off excess.

8. Repeat step 7 for Mrs. Snowman. Glue apple to center front below bodice and above skirt. ❖

Mr. Snowman
37 holes x 68 holes
Cut 1

COLOR KEY	
Worsted Weight Yarn	**Yards**
■ Cherry red #319	10
□ Spring green #367	2
■ Royal #385	3
Uncoded areas are white	
#311 Continental Stitches	20
╱ White #311 Overcasting	
Plastic Canvas Yarn	
■ Black #00	6
■ Maple #13	3
□ Straw #19	1
▨ Gray #38	1
╱ Maple #13 Backstitch	
● Black #00 French Knot	
Rayon Chenille Yarn	
▨ Christmas green #37	2
6-Strand Embroidery Floss	
╱ Black #310 Backstitch	1
╱ Bright orange #608 Straight Stitch	2
╱ Bright Christmas red #666 Backstitch	1
╱ Very light gray green #928 Backstitch	2
● Very light gray green #928 French Knot	
6-Strand Rayon Floss	
╱ Kelly green #30911 Backstitch	3
Satin Ribbon	
╱ Red	1

Color numbers given are for Red Heart Super Saver worsted weight yarn Art. E301, Uniek Needloft plastic canvas yarn, Ruby Mills Honeysuckle Yarns rayon chenille yarn and DMC 6-strand embroidery floss and rayon floss.

COUNTDOWN
TO CHRISTMAS

Design by Joan Green

Stitched in warm, country colors, this pretty stocking helps you count the shopping days left until Christmas!

Skill Level: Beginner

Materials

- 1 sheet 7-count plastic canvas
- Spinrite Bernat Berella "4" worsted weight yarn as listed in color key
- #16 tapestry needle
- Mill Hill Products ceramic buttons from Gay Bowles Sales, Inc.:
  1 gift package #86017
  1 blue present #86098
- Sewing needle and thread to match buttons
- 12" ⅛"-wide red picot-edged satin ribbon
- 12 (⅝") round adhesive-backed hook-and-loop fasteners
- Hot-glue gun

Instructions

1. Cut stocking and hearts from plastic canvas according to graphs (below and page 154).

2. Stitch pieces following graphs, working uncoded area on stocking with hunter green

Continental Stitches and uncoded background on hearts with geranium Continental Stitches.

3. Backstitch line under cuff with dark antique rose. Backstitch numbers on hearts and remainder of letters on stocking with natural. Overcast stocking with hunter green and dark antique rose following graph. Overcast hearts with geranium.

4. Attach buttons to stocking where indicated on graph with sewing

needle and matching thread.

5. Place two rough-sided adhesive-backed hook-and-loop fasteners on stocking where indicated on graph. Place fuzzy-sided adhesive-backed hook-and-loop fasteners on backs of hearts.

6. Using photo as guide, glue ends of satin ribbon to upper corners on backside of stocking for hanger. Place hearts on fastener on stocking. ❖

COLOR KEY	
Worsted Weight Yarn	**Yards**
■ Dark antique rose #8817	3
▨ Geranium #8929	24
☐ Natural #8940	8
Uncoded area on stocking is dark lagoon #8822 Continental Stitches	24
Uncoded areas on hearts are geranium #8929 Continental Stitches	
╱ Hunter green #8931 Overcasting	3
╱ Dark antique rose #8817 Backstitch	
╱ Natural #8940 Backstitch and Straight Stitch	
● Attach button	
● Attach hook-and-loop fastener	
Color numbers given are for Spinrite Bernat Berella "4" worsted weight yarn.	

Countdown to Christmas Hearts
9 holes x 10 holes

Cut 2   Cut 2   Cut 1   Cut 1   Cut 1

Cut 1   Cut 1   Cut 1   Cut 1   Cut 1

COLOR KEY

Worsted Weight Yarn	Yards
■ Dark antique rose #8817	3
▨ Geranium #8929	24
☐ Natural #8940	8
Uncoded area on stocking is dark lagoon #8822 Continental Stitches	24
Uncoded areas on hearts are geranium #8929 Continental Stitches	
⁄ Hunter green #8931 Overcasting	3
⁄ Dark antique rose #8817 Backstitch	
⁄ Natural #8940 Backstitch and Straight Stitch	
● Attach button	
● Attach hook-and-loop fastener	

Color numbers given are for Spinrite Bernat Berella "4" worsted weight yarn.

Countdown to Christmas Stocking
44 holes x 59 holes
Cut 1

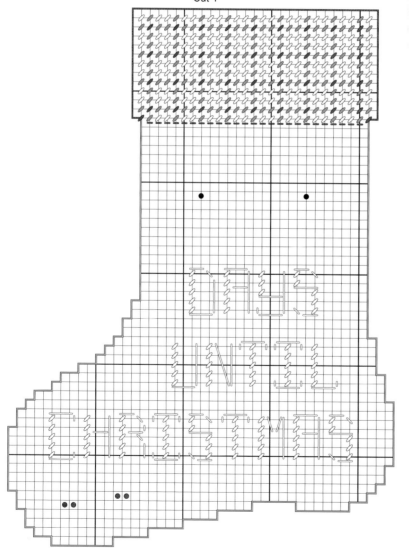

Skill Level: Beginner

Materials

- ½ sheet 7-count plastic canvas
- Red Heart Classic worsted weight yarn Art. E267 as listed in color key
- DMC #3 pearl cotton as listed in color key
- #16 tapestry needle
- 7" each ¼"-wide double-faced satin ribbon: green and wine
- 8" each ⅛"-wide double-faced satin ribbon: green and wine
- ⅝" red heart button
- ⅝" green heart button
- 6 (12mm) mini pine stems
- 4 (3") cinnamon sticks
- Low-temperature glue gun

Instructions

1. Cut plastic canvas according to graphs.

2. Stitch pieces following graphs, reversing one gingerbread man before stitching. Work one pocket front and one back as graphed; work one front and one back, replacing paddy green with light berry. Add Backstitches and French Knots to gingerbread men over completed background stitching.

3. Using eggshell throughout, Overcast gingerbread men and top edges of pocket fronts and backs. Whipstitch wrong sides of corresponding fronts and backs together around side and bottom edges.

4. Using photo as a guide through step 6, thread 2 plies eggshell yarn through each button and tie in back. Tie ¼"-wide green ribbon in a bow; center and glue to front of light berry pocket, then glue red button to center of bow. Repeat with ¼"-wide wine ribbon and green button, gluing to front of paddy green pocket.

5. Thread ends of ⅛"-wide green

GINGERBREAD POCKET ORNAMENTS

Design by Celia Lange Designs

Add this pair of lovable country ornaments to your Christmas tree this year!

ribbon from front to back through top corner holes of light berry pocket back; knot each end and tuck inside pocket. Repeat with ⅛"-wide wine ribbon and paddy green pocket.

6. Glue one gingerbread man in each pocket front. Glue two cinnamon sticks and three pine stems behind each gingerbread man. ❖

COLOR KEY	
Worsted Weight Yarn	**Yards**
☐ Eggshell #111	19
▨ Warm brown #336	6
▨ Paddy green #686	7
☐ Light berry #761	7
#3 Pearl Cotton	
✎ Black #310 Backstitch	1
● Black #310 French Knot	
Color numbers given are for Red Heart Classic worsted weight yarn Art. E267 and DMC #3 pearl cotton.	

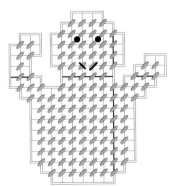

Gingerbread Man
15 holes x 16 holes
Cut 2, reverse 1

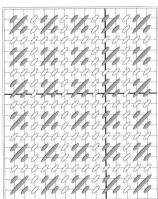

Gingerbread Pocket Front & Back
15 holes x 18 holes
Cut 4
Stitch 2 as graphed
Stitch 2 replacing paddy green
with light berry

Christmas Candle
TISSUE TOPPER
Design by Vicki Blizzard

A colorful wreath of holly circles a brightly burning candle on each side of this Yuletide tissue box cover.

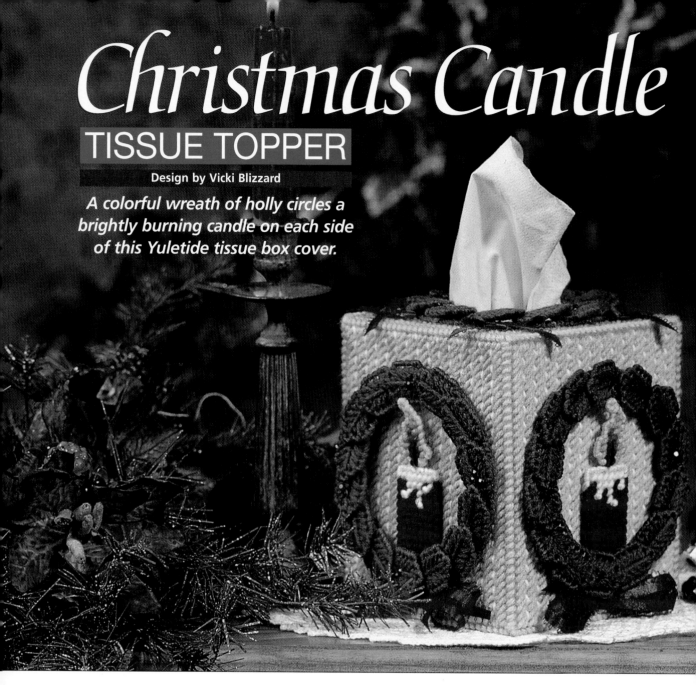

Skill Level: Beginner

Materials

- 2 sheets Uniek Quick-Count 7-count plastic canvas
- 5 (4½") plastic canvas radial circles
- Spinrite plastic canvas yarn as listed in color key
- #18 tapestry needle
- 3⅓ yards ¼"-wide red picot-edge satin ribbon
- 60 (4mm) ruby Austrian crystal rhinestones by National Artcraft
- Hot-glue gun

Instructions

1. Cut sides, top, holly leaves and candles according to graphs. Cut wreath bases following graphs, cutting away gray areas. Wreath bases will remain unstitched.

2. Stitch pieces following graphs. Using 4 plies yarn, work white Running Stitches on sides and top, white French Knots on candles and brisk green Straight Stitches on holly leaves when background stitching is completed. Work Straight Stitches on candles with 2 plies black.

3. Overcast holly leaves and inside and outside edges of wreath bases with brisk green. Overcast candles following graphs. Using almond throughout, Overcast bottom edges of sides and inside edges of top. Whipstitch sides together, then Whipstitch sides to top.

4. Using photo as a guide through step 8 and spacing evenly and overlapping slightly, glue 12 holly leaves to top wreath base. Center and glue wreath to top around opening. Glue three rhinestones to every third leaf. Cut four 6" lengths of red ribbon. Tie each length in a small bow; trim ends. Glue one bow to each corner of top.

5. Spacing evenly and overlapping slightly, glue 14 leaves to one side wreath base. Glue 12 rhinestones in four groups of three to holly leaves.

6. Glue bottom front of one candle to wrong side of wreath, making sure tip of candle flame overlaps top part of wreath slightly. Center and glue wreath to one side.

7. Cut one 18" length and one 6" length of ribbon. Wrap 18" length of ribbon around four fingers of one hand. Slide loops off fingers and tie in center with 6" piece of ribbon; trim ends. Glue

multi-looped bow to tissue cover side directly under wreath.

8. Repeat steps 5–7 for remaining sides of tissue topper. ❖

Tissue Topper Holly Leaf
5 holes x 7 holes
Cut 68

COLOR KEY	
Plastic Canvas Yarn	**Yards**
☐ White #0001	28
▧ Scarlet #0022	1
▣ Brisk green #0027	50
☐ Daffodil #0029	2
▨ Orange #0030	1
■ Crimson #0032	4
▤ Mustard #0043	1
☐ Almond #0056	75
⟋ White #0001 Running Stitch	
⟋ Brisk green #0027 Straight Stitch	
⟋ Black #0028 Straight Stitch	1/3
○ White #0001 French Knot	
Color numbers given are for Spinrite plastic canvas yarn.	

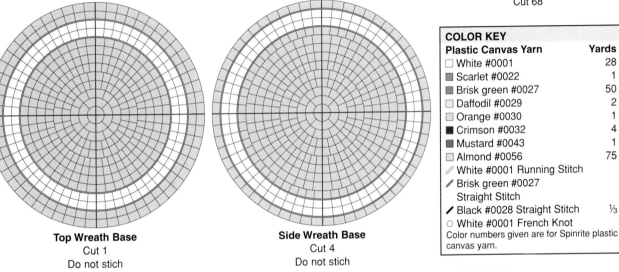

Top Wreath Base
Cut 1
Do not stich

Side Wreath Base
Cut 4
Do not stich

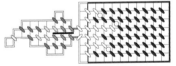

Tissue Topper Candle
7 holes x 20 holes
Cut 4

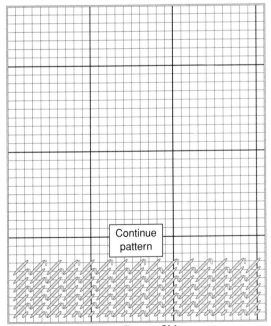

Continue pattern

Tissue Topper Side
31 holes x 37 holes
Cut 4

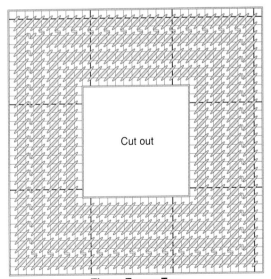

Cut out

Tissue Topper Top
31 holes x 31 holes
Cut 1

Gingerbread

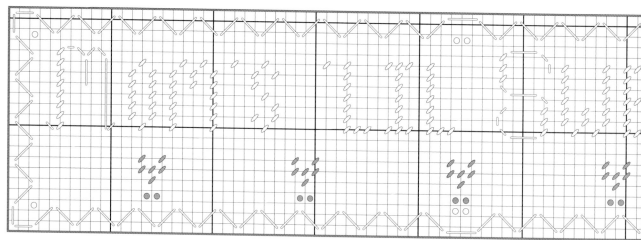

Gingerbread Kids Hanger
88 holes x 21 holes
Cut 1

KIDS

Design by Joan Green

Any mother would be tickled to receive this delightful gift! Three cheerful gingerbread kids make adorable photo frames to capture Mom's favorite school pictures!

COLOR KEY
HANGER

Worsted Weight Yarn	Yards
☐ White	8
▨ Dark pink	1
Uncoded area is light tan Continental Stitches	26
⁄ Dark tan Overcasting	3
⁄ White Backstitch	
○ White French Knot	
● Attach ribbon	

Skill Level: Beginner

Materials

- 7-count plastic canvas:
  ⅓ sheet for hanger
  ⅙ sheet for each cookie frame
- Worsted weight yarn as listed in color key
- #16 tapestry needle
- 10" ⅛"-wide pink satin ribbon for each cookie frame
- Lightweight cardboard
- Sawtooth hanger
- Hot-glue gun

Instructions

1. Cut one hanger and number of cookie frames desired from plastic canvas according to graphs.

2. Stitch pieces following graphs, working uncoded areas with light tan Continental Stitches. Work Backstitches and French Knots when background stitching is completed. Overcast inside and outside edges of cookies and outside edges of hanger with dark tan.

3. Cut one 1¾" x 2⅞" piece from lightweight cardboard for each cookie frame. Center and glue photos on lightweight cardboard; glue cardboard to back of each cookie frame, centering photo in opening.

4. Using photo as a guide throughout, thread ribbon from back to front where indicated under hearts, using third heart for hanging one photo; second and fourth hearts for hanging two photos; and first, third and fifth hearts for hanging three photos. Thread ends of ribbon from back to front through holes indicated on cookie frame; tie in a bow and trim ends as desired. ***Note:*** *Additional frames may be hung from first row of cookie frames.*

5. Glue sawtooth hanger to top center backside of hanger. ❖

COLOR KEY
1 COOKIE FRAME

Worsted Weight Yarn	Yards
■ Dark brown	½
▨ Dark pink	½
Uncoded area is light tan Continental Stitches	7
⁄ Dark tan Overcasting	4
⁄ White Backstitch	2
⁄ Dark brown Backstitch	
● Dark brown French Knot	
● Attach ribbon	

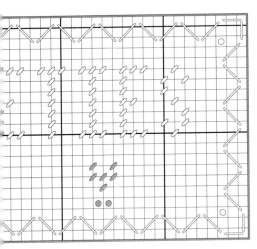

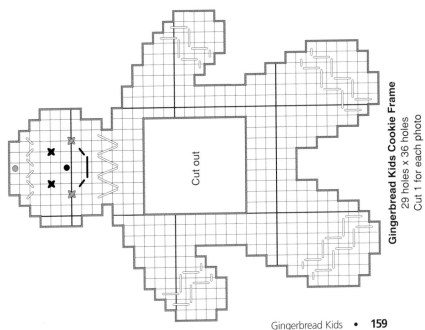

Gingerbread Kids Cookie Frame
29 holes x 36 holes
Cut 1 for each photo

Cut out

Let It S

OW COUNTRY ACCENTS

Designs by Lilo Fruehwirth

Stitch this country-style floor cloth and basket set with cotton fabric strips on five-count plastic canvas for quick and easy home decor.

Skill Level: Intermediate

Materials

- 4 artist-size sheets 5-count plastic canvas
- 45"-wide calico print fabric:
  3 yards navy blue
  ⅛ yard red
  ⅛ yard green
- 45"-wide broadcloth:
  1½ yards white
  1 yard gold
  ⅛ yard turquoise
- #16 tapestry needle
- Sewing needle
- White and gold quilting thread

Project Notes

Cut selvage from fabric. Prepare strips by marking and clipping edges every ¾". Hold fabric firmly at each cut and pull to tear into strips.

Tumble strips in clothes dryer for a few minutes to remove excess lint. Clip loose threads from fabric strips. Wind each color into a ball.

To thread needle, pull one corner of fabric strip through eye of needle. Use short strips when working a small design area.

Floor Cloth

1. Overlap two holes along long edges of two sheets plastic canvas and stitch together with sewing needle and white quilting thread. Cut a 104-hole x 124-hole piece from joined sheets.

2. Stitch floor cloth following graph (page 163), stitching first half of piece to center bar as shown. Turn graph and stitch remaining half. Overcast with gold.

3. For snowmen scarves and hat ties, using colors desired, thread short lengths of fabric strips from back to front through holes indicated on graph with red dots. Tie each in a knot in front as in photo.

Basket

1. Cut one side, two handles and two bottoms from plastic canvas according to graphs.

2. Overlap two holes of basket side edges as indicated on graph and stitch together with sewing needle and white quilting thread; stitch piece following graph. Overcast top edge with gold.

3. Attach short lengths of fabric strips to basket side following step 3 of floor cloth.

4. Place both handle pieces together, matching edges, and both bottom pieces together, matching edges; stitch each as one piece following graphs. Overcast edges on handle and basket bottom with gold.

5. Using sewing needle and gold quilting thread throughout, Whipstitch bottom edges of basket side to basket bottom. Using photo as a guide, place handle edges ½" inside basket side; Backstitch handle to side along top row of holes on basket side. ❖

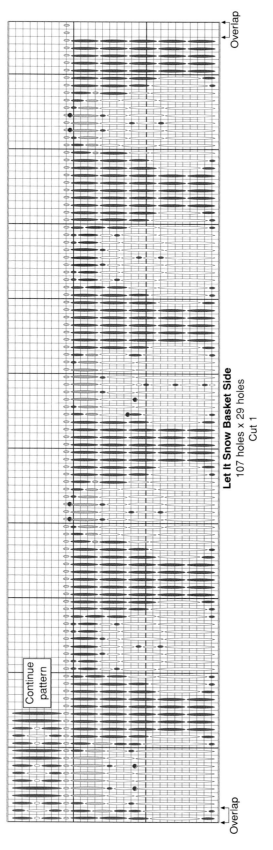

Let It Snow Basket Side
107 holes x 29 holes
Cut 1

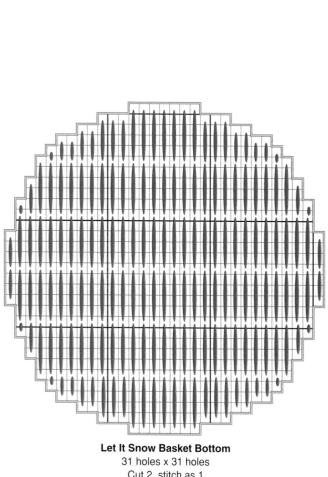

Let It Snow Basket Bottom
31 holes x 31 holes
Cut 2, stitch as 1

COLOR KEY
Calico Print Fabric Strips
■ Navy
■ Red
□ Green
Broadcloth Fabric Strips
□ White
□ Gold
□ Turquoise

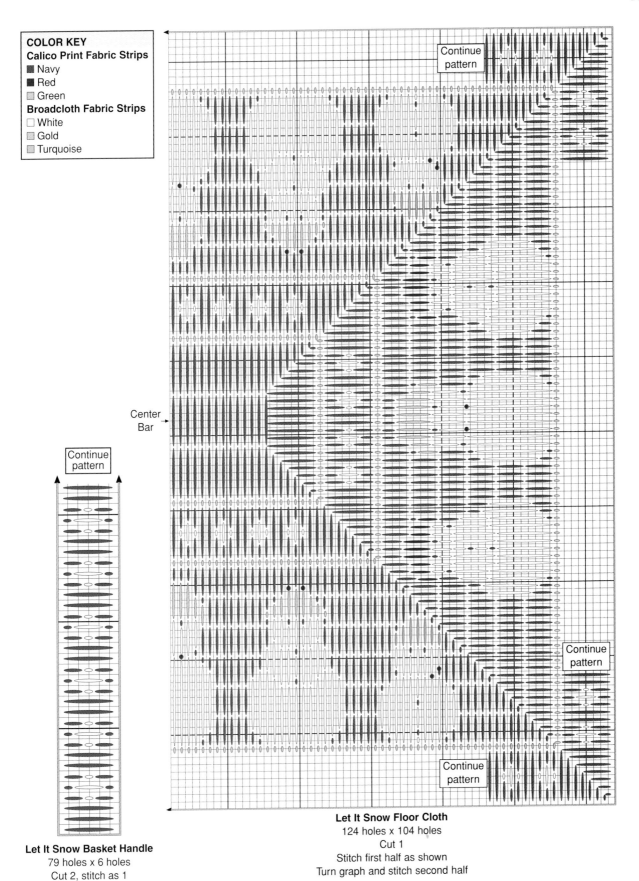

Center Bar →

Continue pattern

Continue pattern

Continue pattern

Continue pattern

Continue pattern

Let It Snow Basket Handle
79 holes x 6 holes
Cut 2, stitch as 1

Let It Snow Floor Cloth
124 holes x 104 holes
Cut 1
Stitch first half as shown
Turn graph and stitch second half

Bargello STOCKING

Design by Darla Fanton

Friends and family will gain a new appreciation for your stitchery when they see this attractive stocking hanging over the mantel!

Skill Level: Beginner

Materials

- 2 (12" x 18") sheets 7-count plastic canvas
- Spinrite Bernat Berella "4" worsted weight yarn as listed in color key
- Madeira Carat 4mm ribbon braid as listed in color key

Instructions

1. Cut plastic canvas according to graphs.

2. Stitch pieces following graphs, reversing back piece before stitching and using a double strand of yarn and a single strand of ribbon braid throughout.

3. Using geranium throughout, Whipstitch gussets to front and back, beginning at top and working down long straight edges, then Whipstitch front and back together around foot area. Overcast top edges.

4. For hanger, thread a 7" length of ribbon braid through center top hole of back gusset. Tie ends in a knot; place knot inside stocking. ❖

COLOR KEY

Worsted Weight Yarn	Yards
☐ Light sea green #8878	18
■ Geranium #8929	58
▨ Hunter green #8981	30
4mm Ribbon Braid	
☐ Gold #425	11

Color numbers given are for Spinrite Bernat
Berella "4" worsted weight yarn and Madeira
Carat 4mm ribbon braid.

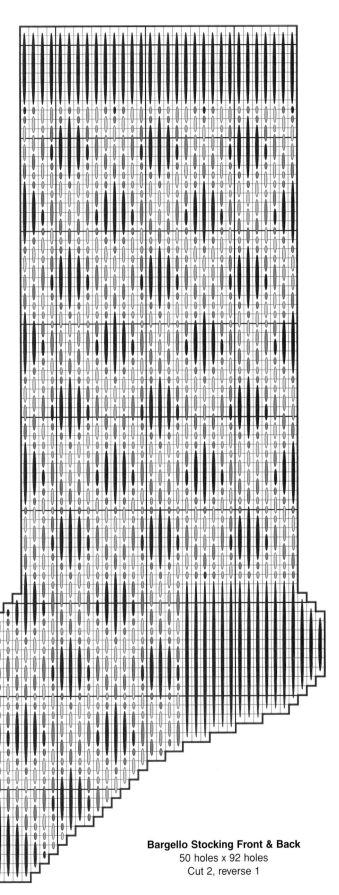

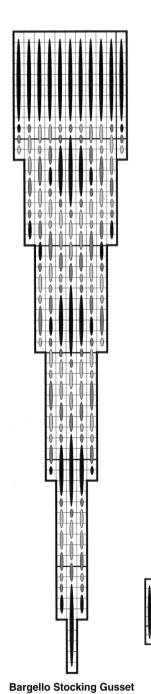

Bargello Stocking Gusset
11 holes x 60 holes
Cut 2

Bargello Stocking Front & Back
50 holes x 92 holes
Cut 2, reverse 1

Snowman Gift Bag

Design by Celia Lange Designs

If you visit friends or family during the holidays, why not take your hostess a thank you gift tucked inside this one-of-a-kind gift bag!

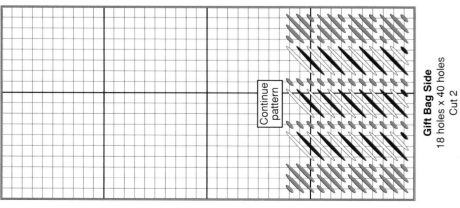

Continue pattern

Gift Bag Side
18 holes x 40 holes
Cut 2

Skill Level: Beginner

Materials

- 2 sheets Darice Ultra-Stiff 7-count plastic canvas
- Red Heart Classic worsted weight yarn Art. E267 as listed in color key
- DMC #3 pearl cotton as listed in color key
- 2 (½") black shank buttons
- 1 red chenille stem
- 1 white chenille stem
- 2 (18mm) oval wiggle eyes
- Scrap orange Fun Foam craft foam by Westrim Crafts
- Black ink pen
- 2 (2") red yarn pompoms
- 12" 1"-wide plaid ribbon
- Low-temperature glue gun

Instructions

1. Cut plastic canvas according to graphs (pages 166–168). Cut one 40-hole x 18-hole piece for bag bottom. Cut one carrot nose from orange craft foam using pattern given. Mark lines on carrot with pen.

2. Stitch pieces following graphs. Continental Stitch bag bottom with paddy green. Overcast head with white and shirt with cherry red. Overcast pocket and top edges of front, back and sides with paddy green.

3. When background stitching and Overcasting are completed, work Backstitches on face and pocket; work double Backstitches on shirt. With black pearl cotton, sew buttons to shirt where indicated on graph.

4. With paddy green, Whipstitch front, back and sides together, then Whipstitch front, back and sides to bottom. Whipstitch wrong sides of two handle pieces together with adjacent colors. Repeat with remaining two pieces.

5. Center and glue handle ends inside basket front and back, making sure top edges of paddy green stitching on handle are even with top edge of bag.

6. Using photo as a guide, through step 9, twist red and white chenille stems together to form candy cane stripe. Cut 1½" off stem and shape into candy cane for pocket.

7. Place candy cane behind pocket, then glue pocket to shirt, making sure bottom edges are even.

8. For scarf, find center of ribbon, then glue center of ribbon along one edge to center back of shirt at neck. Glue shirt to bag with ribbon extended beyond sides. Glue head to bag above shirt at a slight angle, then wrap and tie ribbon around neck. Trim ends in an inverted "V"; glue ribbon tails to shirt.

9. Glue eyes and carrot nose to head. For earmuffs, glue ends of twisted chenille stems to sides of head, then glue pompoms to head and stem ends. ❖

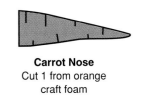

Carrot Nose
Cut 1 from orange
craft foam

COLOR KEY	
Worsted Weight Yarn	**Yards**
☐ White #1	12
■ Black #12	1
▨ Honey gold #645	15
▨ Paddy green #686	49
▨ Lily pink #719	1
■ Cherry red #912	13
▨ Cardinal #917	5
#3 Pearl Cotton	
╱ Black #310 Backstitch	1
● Attach button	
Color numbers given are for Red Heart Classic worsted weight yarn Art. E267 and DMC #3 pearl cotton.	

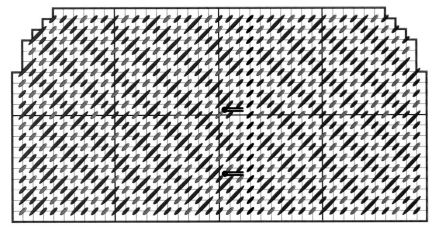

Gift Bag Snowman Shirt
40 holes x 20 holes
Cut 1

Gift Bag Snowman Pocket
7 holes x 8 holes
Cut 1

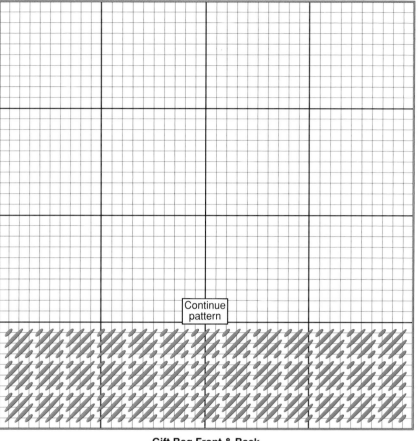

COLOR KEY

Worsted Weight Yarn	Yards
☐ White #1	12
■ Black #12	1
▨ Honey gold #645	15
▨ Paddy green #686	49
☐ Lily pink #719	1
■ Cherry red #912	13
▨ Cardinal #917	5

#3 Pearl Cotton

✓ Black #310 Backstitch	1
● Attach button	

Color numbers given are for Red Heart
Classic worsted weight yarn Art. E267
and DMC #3 pearl cotton.

Gift Bag Front & Back
40 holes x 40 holes
Cut 2

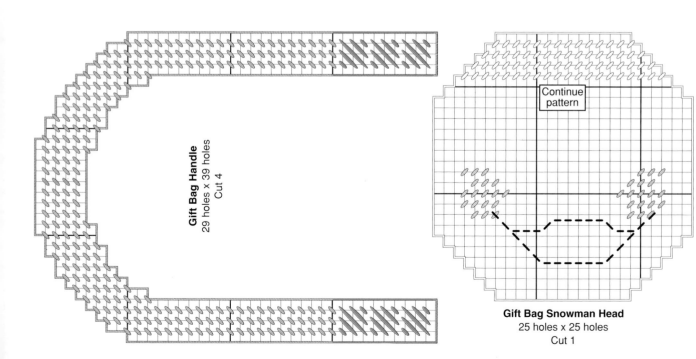

Gift Bag Handle
29 holes x 39 holes
Cut 4

Gift Bag Snowman Head
25 holes x 25 holes
Cut 1

TEDDY BEAR
Christmas

As they ride upon their rocking horse and unicorn, these holiday bears will add precious charm to your Christmas tree!

Designs by Angie Arickx

Skill Level: Beginner

Materials
- ⅓ sheet 7-count plastic canvas
- Uniek Needloft plastic canvas yarn as listed in color key
- #16 tapestry needle
- 2 (1½") flocked Santa bears
- Monofilament (optional)
- Hot-glue gun

Instructions
1. Cut plastic canvas according to graphs.

2. Following graphs throughout, stitch saddle tops and runner bases. Stitch rocking pieces, reversing one piece for each decoration before stitching, then stitch in a mirror image. Work French Knot eyes when background stitching is completed.

3. With Christmas red, Whipstitch long edges of one base to bottom edge of runners on rocking horse from blue dot to blue dot. Whipstitch saddle top to saddles on rocking pieces with holly. Overcast remaining edges following graphs. Repeat for rocking unicorn.

4. Using photo as a guide, glue Santa bears to saddles. If desired, thread monofilament through holes on finished pieces; tie ends in a knot for hanging. ❖

COLOR KEY	
Plastic Canvas Yarn	**Yards**
■ Christmas red #02	7
■ Maple #13	4
■ Holly #27	3
□ White #41	4
✎ Brown #15 Overcasting	3
✎ Gold #17 Overcasting	1
✎ Gray #38 Overcasting	3
● Brown #15 French Knot	
○ Gray #38 French Knot	
Color numbers given are for Uniek Needloft plastic canvas yarn.	

Saddle Top
5 holes x 5 holes
Cut 2

Runner Base
12 holes x 12 holes
Cut 2

Rocking Unicorn
20 holes x 24 holes
Cut 2, reverse 1

Rocking Horse
20 holes x 24 holes
Cut 2, reverse 1

"Dear Santa" MAG

Tell Santa if you've been naughty or nice this year with this whimsical Christmas magnet! Take it to the office for more holiday fun!

JET

Design by Vicki Blizzard

Skill Level: Intermediate

Materials

- ½ sheet Uniek Quick-Count clear 7-count plastic canvas
- Small amount Uniek Quick-Count white 7-count plastic canvas
- Spinrite plastic canvas yarn as listed in color key
- #18 tapestry needle
- 6" ⅛"-wide green satin ribbon
- 2 (6mm) round black cabochons by The Beadery
- 7mm round frosted ruby cabochon by The Beadery
- 5 (11.5mm) heart cabochons by The Beadery
- 9mm white jingle bell
- 4 (7mm) gold jump rings
- Gold cup hook
- 4 (½") magnet buttons
- Needle-nose pliers
- Hot-glue gun

Cutting & Stitching

1. Cut Santa sign back from white plastic canvas; cut Santa sign front and remaining pieces from clear plastic canvas according to graphs (page 172).

2. Stitch pieces following graphs, working uncoded areas on signs and beard area on face with white Continental Stitches. Over completed background stitching, work letters on top line of naughty sign with 2 plies scarlet and on top line of nice sign with 2 plies brisk green. Work all other embroidery with 4 plies yarn.

3. Whipstitch wrong sides of Santa sign front and Santa sign back together with scarlet and white, alternating colors to form a candy cane effect.

4. Whipstitch wrong sides of naughty and nice signs together with scarlet and white, alternating colors as with Santa sign.

5. Overcast Santa face and mustache with white. Overcast Santa hat tip with scarlet. Overcast Santa hat with scarlet and white following graph.

6. Using brisk green throughout, Overcast two leaves; set aside for Santa sign. Whipstitch wrong sides of two leaves together, then repeat with remaining two leaves; set aside for use on naughty-and-nice sign.

Assembly

1. Using photo as a guide throughout assembly, push Whipstitching aside and insert cup hook where indicated on Santa sign graph, using a screwing motion to ease hook between front and back pieces. Glue one magnet button to each corner on back of Santa sign.

2. Using needle-nose pliers, insert one jump ring in each hole marked with blue dot on naughty-and-nice sign. Attach a third jump ring through both jump rings and close to form a hanger.

3. Center and glue the two Whipstitched pairs of leaves to bottom of naughty-and-nice sign. Glue one heart cabochon to center top of leaf cluster on both sides of leaves. Glue one heart cabochon on left side of nice sign and one on right side of nice sign.

4. Attach remaining jump ring to hole indicated with blue dot on Santa hat tip. Insert jump ring through bell, then pinch closed with needle-nose pliers. Tie green ribbon in a tiny bow; trim ends. Glue bow to hat tip over jump ring.

5. Glue top edge of hat tip to top edge of hat. Glue black cabochons to face under white eyebrows. Glue frosted ruby cabochon to face where indicated for nose. Glue mustache to face directly under nose. Glue hat to top of head.

6. Glue completed Santa face to right side of Santa sign at a slight angle. Glue the two Overcast leaves to sign between Santa and the word "DEAR." Glue remaining heart cabochon to leaves.

7. Slip hanger jump ring on sign onto cup hook. ❖

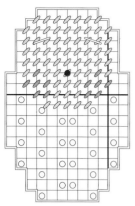

Magnet Santa Face
12 holes x 18 holes
Cut 1 from clear

COLOR KEY

Plastic Canvas Yarn	Yards
☐ White #0001	22
☐ Pale pink #0003	2
☐ Cherry blossom #0010	1
■ Scarlet #0022	5
■ Brisk green #0027	6

Uncoded areas are white
#0001 Continental Stitches
⁄ White #0001 Straight Stitch
⁄ Scarlet #0022 Backstitch
⁄ Brisk green #0027 Backstitch
and Straight Stitch
○ White #0001 French Knot
● Brisk green #0027 French Knot
● Attach frosted ruby cabochon
Color numbers given are for Spinrite plastic
canvas yarn.

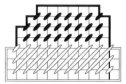

Magnet Santa Mustache
17 holes x 6 holes
Cut 1 from clear

Magnet Santa Hat
11 holes x 7 holes
Cut 1 from clear

Magnet Santa Hat Tip
5 holes x 9 holes
Cut 1 from clear

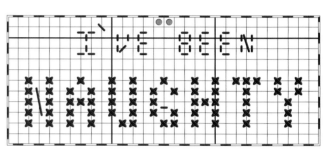

Magnet Naughty Sign
30 holes x 12 holes
Cut 1 from clear

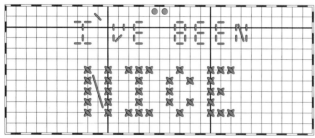

Magnet Nice Sign
30 holes x 12 holes
Cut 1 from clear

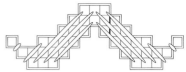

Magnet Leaf
5 holes x 6 holes
Cut 6 from clear

Magnet Santa Sign
43 holes x 18 holes
Cut 1 from clear for front
Stitch as graphed
Cut 1 from white for back
Do not stitch

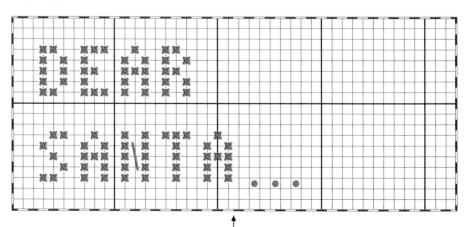

Insert cup hook

Shopper's Guide

Special thanks to the following manufacturers who provided the designers with product with which to work. To find materials listed, first check your local craft and retail stores. If you are unable to locate a product locally, contact the manufacturers below for the closest retail source in your area.

THE BEADERY
105 Canonchet Rd.,
P.O. Box 178
Hope Valley, RI 02832
(401) 539-2432

BUCILLA CORP.
1 Oak Ridge Rd.
Humboldt Industrial Park
Hazelton, PA 18201
(717) 384-2525

COATS & CLARK
30 Patewood Dr., Suite 351
Greenville, SC 29615
(864) 234-0331

CRAFTER'S PRIDE
Daniel Enterprises
306 McKay St.,
P.O. Box 1105
Laurinburg, NC 28352
(910) 277-7441

DARICE, INC.
Mail Order Source:
Bolek's
330 N. Tuscarawas Ave.
Dover, OH 44622
(330) 364-8878

DMC Corp.
10 Port Kearny
South Kearny,
NJ 07032
(201) 589-0606

KREINIK MFG. CO. INC.
3601 Timanus Ln.,
Suite 101
Baltimore, MD 21244
(800) 537-2166

MADEIRA MARKETING, INC.
600 E. Ninth
Michigan City, IN 46360
(219) 873-1000

MILL HILL
Gay Bowles Sales, Inc.
P.O. Box 1060
Janesville, WI 53545
(800) 447-1332

NATIONAL ARTCRAFT
7996 Darrow Rd.
Twinsburg, OH 44087
(888) 937-2723

ONE & ONLY CREATIONS
P.O. Box 2730
Napa, CA 94558
(707) 255-8033

RAINBOW GALLERY
Mail Order Source:
Designs by Joan Green
6345 Fairfield Rd.
Oxford, OH 45056
(513) 523-2690

SPINRITE, INC.
Box 40
Listowel, Ontario N4W
3H3 Canada
(519) 291-3780

UNIEK, INC.
Mail Order Source:
The Needlecraft Shop
23 Old Pecan Rd.
Big Sandy, TX 75755
(800) 259-4000

WESTRIM CRAFTS
9667 Canoga Ave.
P.O. Box 3879
Chatsworth, CA 91313
(800) 727-2727

Stitch Guide

Use the following diagrams to expand your plastic canvas stitching. For each diagram, bring needle up through canvas at the red number one and go back down through the canvas at the red number two. The second stitch is numbered in green. Always bring needle up through the canvas at odd numbers and take it back down through the canvas at the even numbers.

Background Stitches

The following stitches are used for filling in large areas of canvas. The Continental Stitch is the most commonly used stitch. Other stitches, such as the Condensed Mosaic and Scotch Stitch, fill in large areas of canvas more quickly than the Continental Stitch because their stitches cover a larger area of canvas.

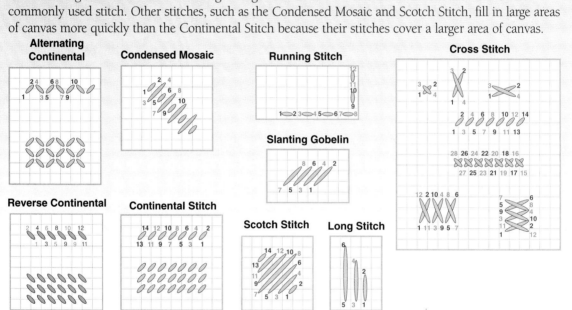

Embroidery Stitches

Embroidery stitches are worked on top of a stitched area to add detail and beauty to your project. Embroidery stitches are usually worked with one strand of yarn, several strands of pearl cotton or several strands of embroidery floss.

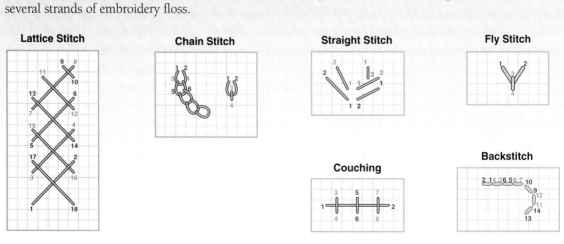

Embroidery Stitches

French Knot

Bring needle up through piece. Wrap yarn around needle 2 or 3 times, depending on desired size of knot; take needle back through piece through same hole.

Lazy Daisy

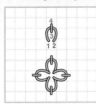

Bring yarn needle up through canvas, then back down in same hole, leaving a small loop.

Then, bring needle up inside loop; take needle back down through piece on other side of loop.

Specialty Stitches

The following stitches can be worked either on top of a previously stitched area or directly onto the canvas. Like the embroidery stitches, these too add wonderful detail and give your stitching additional interest and texture.

Diamond Eyelet

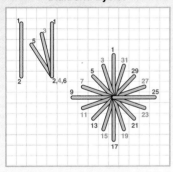

For each stitch, bring needle up at odd numbers around outside and take needle down through canvas at center hole.

Smyrna Cross

Satin Stitch

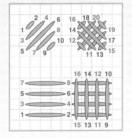

This stitch gives a "padded" look to your work.

Finishing Stitches

Both of these stitches are used to finish the outer edges of the canvas. Overcasting is done to finish one edge at a time. Whipstitch is used to stitch two pieces of canvas together. For both Overcasting and Whip-stitching, work one stitch in each hole along straight edges and inside corners, and two or three stitches in outside corners.

Overcast/Whipstitch

Loop Stitch or Turkey Loop Stitch

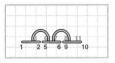

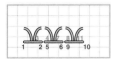

The top diagram shows this stitch left intact. This is an effective stitch for giving a project dimensional hair. The bottom diagram demonstrates the cut loop stitch. Because each stitch is anchored, cutting it will not cause the stitches to come out. A group of cut loop stitches gives a fluffy, soft look and feel to your project.

Special Thanks

We would like to give special thanks and acknowledgment to the following designers whose work is published in this book.

Angie Arickx
Decorative Easter Eggs, Easter Cross Ornaments, Menorah Gift Box, New Year's Noisemakers, Pastel Hearts, Star of David, Teddy Bear Christmas, Teddy Bear Cupid, Top o' the Mornin' Magnet

Vicki Blizzard
Best Witches, Bless Our Irish Home, Christmas Candle Tissue Topper, "Dear Santa" Magnet, Devotional Cross, Hogs 'n' Kisses, Kiss Me Not, Leprechaun Pin, Patriotic Welcome, Peaceful Doves Doily, Precious Pet Treat Baskets, Stars & Stripes Picnic Set, Thanksgiving Angel, Through the Seasons, Tulip Garden, Tulip Time, Witch's Brew Centerpiece

Janna Britton
Mr. & Mrs. Snowman

Celia Lange & Martha Bleidner of Celia Lange Designs
Autumn Florals Centerpiece, Gingerbread Pocket Ornaments,

Halloween Graveyard, Mini Candy Bag, Mother's Sampler, Pot o' Gold Favor, Pumpkin Patch, Rocket Centerpiece, Shalom Vase, Snowman Gift Bag, Thanksgiving Nut Cups (Indian Nut Cup)

Mary T. Cosgrove
New Year's Fridgies

Darla Fanton
Bargello Stocking

Lilo Fruehwirth
Let It Snow Country Accents

Joan Green
Countdown to Christmas, Easter Basket Tissue Topper, Gingerbread Kids, Halloween Shelf Sitters

Robin Howard-Will
Celebration Banners, Harvesttime Bread Basket

Judi Kauffman
Bunny Bookmark, Spring Veggies

Nancy Marshall
Spooky Napkin Rings,

Thanksgiving Nut Cups (Turkey Nut Cup)

Carol Nartowicz
Bless the Irish, Celebration Sign, Pinecone Welcome Wreath, Scarecrow Centerpiece

Kathleen Marie O'Donnell
Floral Nosegay

Kimberly A. Suber
Metallic Heart Wreath, Sweetheart Frame

Ruby Thacker
Arrowhead Desk Set, Handy Can Covers

Brandon J. Wiant
Mom & Dad Beverage Sets

Michele Wilcox
Conversation Hearts Basket, Trick or Treat Bag

Kathy Wirth
Pocket Coasters

> **Also a special thanks to our cover models, Tiffany and Alexis Johnston.**